THE PRODUCT MARKETING MANAGER

Responsibilities and Best Practices
in a Technology Company

LUCAS WEBER

About the Author

Lucas Weber began his career as a Software Product Manager until finding his calling as a Software Product Marketing Manager, which utilizes his talents for communicating development "tech talk" into marketing and sales messaging and for positioning a product for success in companies of all sizes.

TABLE OF
CONTENTS

INTRODUCTION

"What will you be doing here?" asked my new colleague during my first week at a small company I had recently joined as its very first Product Marketing Manager (PMM). He was a developer and explained that, to his understanding, everyone who worked in marketing was there to market the company's products so why would someone be hired with a redundant title like mine? What would I be doing for this company that wasn't already being done?

Having faced this same situation at multiple companies in the past, I had a ready answer: "Defining the positioning and messaging of our products as well as planning and executing product releases and launches."

Although he seemed somewhat satisfied with my answer, I had the feeling that he still didn't clearly understand the role of a PMM. Could I blame him? That one sentence could never explain all of the intricacies of the role.

I decided to search online for a book that best explained the role. To my surprise, I was not able to find what I was looking for. Sure, there were a few books that touched briefly on the subject or offered quotes from successful professionals who had worked in the role, but nothing that succinctly and clearly tied everything together and was also entertaining to read. That quest is what led to the creation of this book.

Before we jump into it, I should begin by explaining a bit about myself and my experience in the role. My background is in software product management: helping to create and deliver the best possible products and sustainable revenue growth as a Product Manager (PM). While I was successful and happy in this field (advancing from PM to Director of Product Management with my own team of PMs), I noticed over the years that my most valuable talent was actually in product positioning and messaging.

When it came to understanding a product on the technical level and then turning that detailed information into key marketing and sales messages by defining a unique selling proposition and differentiation from competition, I was suddenly enjoying my daily work more than ever before.

I left product management to join another company as a Senior PMM. No longer was I working in teams of programmers and PMs but was now fully immersed in a marketing team. This new group had its own terminology, perspectives, tasks, and workflows, much of which was new to me.

I briefly searched for a book about the PMM role when I made this switch. However, I must have been rather caught up in learning-by-doing because the desire for a good book on the subject was soon forgotten amidst other topics.

Since that time, I have spent many years thoroughly enjoying the PMM role and working alongside others similar to me, be they colleagues of mine or people from other companies whom I have interviewed for their insights or worked alongside in different projects.

I have also witnessed numerous times that there is no clear path to becoming a PMM. There are no standardized lessons, classes, or degrees that would be universally recognized and accepted. This is because the role and responsibilities of the PMM varies from professional to professional and from company to company. The path to product marketing can have many beginnings and PMMs come from different educational backgrounds and experiences. Perhaps you studied Computer Science, Literature, History, Economics, or received your degree in Business Administration. You may have come from working in Product or Project Management, Marketing Communications, Programming, Sales, or any number of other roles. What is important is that you arrived at product marketing because it is what inspires and drives you and because you add the most value to your organization in that particular role. If you are still considering if this role is right for you, this book will help you decide.

While it touches upon a wide range of topics, this book focuses solely upon those topics from a PMM's perspective and defines them as part of the role. There may be many tasks and responsibilities in this book that speak directly to you and yet there may be some that you choose to ignore as they are not relevant to you or your company at this time. Part of the pleasure of being a PMM is defining and adapting the role to match your personal strengths as well as aligning it with your company's needs.

As part of my pursuit of excellence and desire to learn more about the role, I have attended numerous presentations about the subject and completed the most popular and useful training courses and certifications available. While these courses are valuable and highly recommended, they tend to focus on what the role means on a conceptual level but not what is required of it on a more practical level. This book closes that gap and provides practical examples of everyday situations and tasks associated with the role of the PMM to further your understanding of how to apply what you know.

I have drawn upon my personal experiences to illustrate this book, but have also incorporated experiences, anecdotes, and feedback from other professionals I have worked with. My hope is that this book provides insights into this wonderful role and that every reader comes away with a better understanding of, and desire to become proficient in, Product Marketing.

I

THE HYBRID ROLE

The Communicator

There is an often-cited quote that states that regardless of what job you have, your ultimate success will be based upon your academic credentials (5%), your professional experiences (15%), and your communication skills (80%).

It could be easily argued that for a PMM, the balance is even more heavily weighted towards communication. A good PMM needs to embrace communication as the key to obtaining the best results both internally within their company and externally. This includes controlling the incoming and outgoing flow of information, how it is filtered and captured, organized, and communicated further.

When it comes to the intake of information, being a PMM means conducting constant research and absorbing the most relevant and important data. As we delve deeper into how the PMM interacts with different business units within the company, and ultimately how successful product positioning and messaging is accomplished, we will see that one must keep alert at all times. Examples include attending industry events, meeting prospects and customers, conducting surveys, and tapping into social media.

It may begin to seem like an impossible amount of data that the PMM must gather and an equally impossible amount of tasks to complete and meetings to attend. Just like any role in an organization, we cannot accomplish everything at once but we can identify where we can make the greatest impact at any given time and what data will help get us there. Good prioritization skills and management of one's time and focus is the solution. Even though PMMs work with many business units simultaneously, we must often prioritize which meetings and projects we have time for and which can be handled by other people who can relay the most relevant information to us at a later time.

I have often found myself overwhelmed with data but the solution is quite simple: Which of that data do you currently need right now and what can wait for later (or never)? A PMM must gather as much information as possible and then filter out what is not relevant. Some of that filtered information may be useful later but are you equipped to handle it at this moment and is it relevant to the tasks at hand? Filtering also means accepting different (sometimes exceptionally different) perspectives and messages from different stakeholders and assimilating them into a greater understanding.

Let's first look at collecting information from within your organization. If you reach out to someone in Sales to better understand what your prospects are asking for and responding to, the answer will most likely be weighted towards conversations they most recently had with prospective clients, rather than from a more general point-of-view.

If you ask a developer in your company about a product's functionality, they may complain about what the product cannot do, rather than boast about what it can do. Their answers may seem negative but most likely they are quite proud of the product. Only because they don't need to directly sell it themselves have they already moved on mentally to where the product should be in six months time.

When looking outside of your organization for information, speaking directly with customers is a natural starting point. When speaking one-on-one with a customer, he or she may answer your questions honestly and in detail but if your questions were not properly prepared or well thought-out, the answers may not reveal the customer's true intellectual and emotional decision-making processes. Additionally, their answers will most likely tell you the "What" of what they are searching for but not the "Why". To understand the problems they are really trying to solve, keep pushing for the "Why". We will cover this more in a later chapter.

Collecting data from outside of your organization can be difficult and may require a clever twist. As an example, I often receive emails from the companies whose products I use. In these emails, I am asked to respond to surveys that will provide these companies with information that will help them improve both my user experience and their understanding of who uses their product, as well as how and why. I almost always respond to these types of surveys as I am interested in what questions they ask and how the questions are phrased. Most assuredly, a PMM was involved in their creation.

I have noticed on many occasions that these companies need an additional hook to draw enough results. Typically, the emails entice the recipients to respond to the survey by offering something such as, "By responding to this survey, your name will automatically be added in a raffle for a chance to win a new tablet!" I still haven't won any prizes but learning from their surveys has provided enough of a reward, especially when those companies are in the same industry as I am.

Keeping up with the trends and developments in your industry is vital. Without knowing the direction of your industry, how your competitors are positioning themselves, or what the demands of your market are, producing a strategy and successful product positioning simply isn't possible.

An easy way to listen to what your customers and the market are talking about is to use social media. For example, set alerts for when someone mentions your company in an article or blog post. Additionally, ask someone in your marketing team to routinely send you a list of the most common keywords people search for before they land on your website. Keyword planning tools are also incredibly effective for finding which keywords are most relevant to your business or product. Passive listening can be a very useful tool and source of inspiration.

Finally, do your best to avoid your own biases when listening to what others have to say or think. I must admit that I have at times been guilty of this myself. For example, I might have spoken to ten people about finding the exact words that should be used to describe a certain product and received the same answer from all of them. However, when speaking with an eleventh person who had a different (but valid) opinion, I have felt that the research had already been successfully completed and the decision made even though this final person had some valuable insights. Having identified this perilous trap, I now keep an open mind when collecting information throughout all phases of a project and remind myself that product positioning and messaging are constantly changing as products, technologies, and markets evolve.

I remember when a PMM colleague had completed copious amounts of research and decided upon a new product positioning that she was going to present to our management team the next week. A few days before the meeting, she and I were engaged in a conversation with a salesperson who articulated his own version of the positioning in a much more effective way than what she had prepared. I watched her ego struggle with adopting that last minute change even though it had the potential to vastly improve her presentation. I was proud to see her accept the suggestions and her final proposal was indeed enthusiastically received by the management team.

Keeping your ego in check is easier if you constantly remind yourself that as a PMM, it is your job to discover, compile, and propose new positioning and messaging, regardless of its source. Although it would be wonderful if it were the PMM who always came up with the latest and greatest messaging to describe the company's products and offering, outside input is a necessity. Listening with an open mind to those who have worked in the company or industry longer than you may very well produce the results that you are looking for, or at the very least, help you on your journey to get there. While there may be great ideas and experience in the team, no one but the PMM is going to spend time digging it out and piecing it all together. Even if your new messaging were to be solely created by interviewing colleagues and customers, there is much pride in being the one who was able to clearly and succinctly articulate the collective voices and opinions. Collecting detailed information, understanding what people mean but may or may not say, and keeping an eye on the big picture is the true test of a PMM.

When it comes to the dissemination of information, PMMs may be called upon to write blogs, speak at trade shows, update colleagues with new information and plans, communicate the best product messaging to audiences at the right times through the right channels, and much more. Both spoken and written communication are crucial to a successful career in product marketing.

The Storyteller

So is there a trick to it all? Is there a simple way of defining how a PMM uses all of that available information to dramatically increase their product sales? Indeed, I would argue that there is: Good storytelling.

Whether you are marketing physical goods or software, it is humans, not robots, who are making the decisions to purchase, and we must therefore appeal to their emotional, as well as to their intellectual, decision-making processes. Keep this in mind when speaking both internally within your organization and externally.

Oftentimes we must sell a new product or feature internally to our own Sales team before they will see the benefit in selling it to their prospects. If they don't feel comfortable selling it by themselves without assistance or don't believe that it adds value to their sales pitch or has the potential to increase their monthly commission bonus, why would they spend time with it? They could just as easily continue to reach their sales targets with the other products they have already been selling successfully for years. One useful approach that I have witnessed is to record one of the company's top performing salespeople delivering the pitch for that particular product or feature. After the other salespeople watch the recording, they will see the value and approach to selling it and will do their best to emulate that example. This can be extended to identifying and marketing product champions or evangelists within your company to help represent and promote certain products. The same principle applies to any business unit that interacts with customers and prospects. Crafting and selling the story internally is just as important as selling it externally.

As clarification, when I refer to "Sales" or a "salesperson", I am speaking about all roles that handle direct sales, be it new sales to prospects or upsales to existing customers. Therefore, the "salesperson" term includes other roles and titles such as, Sales Managers, Business Development Managers, Customer Success Managers, Account Managers, Presales, etc.

Occasionally we must identify value where there appears to be none. As an example, when a minor release of your product becomes available, your Sales team may not pay attention to it because it "only contains bug fixes". How can you turn these bug fixes into a compelling reason for them to care? With a bit of research, you may find out that one of these bug fixes affects 80% of your customer base. Isn't that a good reason for a salesperson to reach out to an existing customer to convey the positive message that the bug is now fixed, ask how they are doing otherwise, and perhaps use the opportunity to upsell another product at the same time?

In many companies, this internal product evangelism is handled by PMs. However, the PM's focus is on the product itself, including its features, usability, and roadmap. The PMM enforces the PM's message by bringing the sales and customer benefits to the forefront. Namely, why should someone be interested in the product? To tell a truly great story, the PMM and PM must work together.

The best explanation I have heard for the difference between a PM and PMM is that it is the PM's job to get a product onto the shelf, while it is the PMM's job to get it off the shelf. In other words, the PM is focused on developing the best product possible while the PMM is focused on getting it sold. If PMs play the role of product evangelists within the organization, PMMs play the role outside of the organization. While PMs focus on developing, improving, and championing their products internally, it is the PMMs who package every product attractively and deliver persuasive arguments for external interest and motivation to purchase.

This is where good storytelling comes into play. The ability to put oneself into the shoes of the buyers, understand what will interest them and what they will respond to, and then relate information to them in an easy to understand and attractive manner is what sets good PMMs apart from the crowd.

Think about it this way: If the roles were reversed and you were the prospective client who was reading or listening to the PMM's story, would it excite or interest you? Would it speak directly to the problems that you are hoping to solve as if the story had been tailored specifically to you and your needs? Would it leave you wanting more and with an enticing call to action? Master the ability to tell a good story around a product and everything else will fall into place.

Nothing beats testing your story like a good dialogue. Speaking directly with prospects and customers will challenge you and your story in more ways than one. Rarely have I had a conversation in which I was not asked a product-related question which made me wonder why the answer was not already readily apparent in our marketing material or why it was so difficult for me to produce the same answer as one of my colleagues. Many times, the inadequacy of the marketing material is the result of the marketing team not spending enough time with prospects and customers and becoming familiar with their frequently asked questions. Taking advantage of opportunities to interact directly with customers and prospects is the best way to hone your story and create the right material necessary to back it up.

However, a customer's own words to explain why your product works so well for them can be even more powerful than telling your own story. Using your customer's comments about how your products have helped them is an effective and powerful tool to add interest and credibility to your story. If you have satisfied customers, why not nurture them into becoming advocates and evangelists for your brand by giving them a platform to promote your products? Invite them to speak at a conference, ask them to be a guest writer on your company's blog, or set up another online outlet for them to express how you solved their problems and converted them into advocates of your products.

Additionally, happy customers who have experienced great results will very often be willing to become documented success stories that you can share with your prospects. The more customers talk about how your products have helped them, the stronger and more persuasive your story becomes.

The Public Speaker

Public speaking is another good place to begin honing your storytelling abilities. Many companies value presentation skills in their employees and are more than happy to pay for external training to foster it.

When explaining a product or topic to an audience, be sure to leave them with something memorable, even if it is just a single phrase, statement, or question. You may be the only presenter they hear that day or the tenth. What matters is that you capture their attention and use good storytelling to tie their interest in your speech to what you have to say about your product. Think back to the best presentations you have ever heard. Chances are, they were both engaging and entertaining. Perhaps tell a story about something personal that happened to you or your company or something else that the audience can relate to.

I have always loved delivering public speeches and many of my colleagues over the years have asked me for hints and tips on how to feel more comfortable on stage. The next question from them is invariably, "What about when you have to speak about a boring subject?" Although they may or may not believe my answer, I reply that there is no such thing as a boring subject so long as it is made to be entertaining. As a PMM, I relish the challenge of taking a difficult subject and turning it into a memorable story.

As an example, I once flew to Lithuania to speak at a conference about network virtualization. With a topic like that, you cannot assume that everyone in the audience has a full grasp of the concept, even when attending an event dedicated to virtualization. Perhaps some of the audience members are new to it and are there to learn. Perhaps others are already very familiar with it but have not thought about certain aspects of it. There might even be someone in the audience who already knows everything you are going to speak about but will nevertheless be open to an entertaining version of it.

For my speech that particular time, I used a hamburger analogy to explain how network virtualization works. I told a personal story of how I had been out to lunch with my colleagues when I came up with the analogy and it helped the audience relate to me as a presenter. My goal was to clearly explain my subject in an entertaining way, stand out from the other presenters, and have my audience remember my message and key points. While waiting for my flight home in the airport lounge later that evening, I was approached by a group of the event's attendees who wanted to thank me for my speech and to ask more about my company's product.

Webinars are another important form of public speaking. While webinars are generally about educating an audience on a specific topic, they can also be used to speak to the benefits of a specific product or company. Usually, the product-specific information is delivered at the end of a webinar as a solution to the identified problem.

Delivering the webinar yourself is also a useful method for perfecting your messaging and collecting feedback. As with sitting in front of a prospect and convincing them of the power of your product, hosting a webinar will put you directly in the spotlight and require that you have your pitch well prepared. Instead of coordinating a webinar and then outsourcing the hosting to someone else, take it upon yourself to be the voice of your company. Practice with the presentation multiple times before you go live and you will see that repetition allows you to improve that particular presentation as well as gain perspective on your overall messaging. After the webinar is over, send out a feedback survey for suggestions on how you can improve for next time.

Although I have often heard the argument that one of the company's star salespeople should host the webinar to ensure the best sales pitch, doesn't it make sense to have the host be the person from whom the sales pitch originates? After all, the sales team may represent the company and its products for a living but it is the PMM who provides the information and messaging about the company and products to the sales team. Additionally, if the webinar's focus should be more educational and less of a sales pitch, a salesperson will usually have trouble staying away from the sales aspect, whereas the PMM can serve more as an industry expert. If we are unable to host a successful webinar on our own as a PMM, perhaps our messaging isn't as strong as it should be or we are not practiced enough at delivering it. If we cannot clearly define and articulate the values and benefits of our company and products, how can we expect anyone else to?

The Leader

When it comes to communication, speaking with customers and prospects and publicly positioning your products is only half the battle. Communicating within your organization is where the journey begins.

The PMM must assume the role of a leader. You must be prepared to ask the "stupid" questions to ensure that everyone has the same understanding of the subject and/or explanation. This will be an invaluable time saver later when you don't have to reeducate the same people again and it will be appreciated by the listeners who were too timid to ask the question on their own. Sometimes, to create a safe environment in a situation in which I am not sure that everyone has understood the same message delivered by a colleague, it works to say, "I only spend part of my time with development/sales/marketing (take your pick) and therefore don't understand it completely. Can you please explain it to me as if I am brand new to this subject?"

It finally reached a point where I feel absolutely zero embarrassment for asking a question so long as I know that it needs to be asked. Alternatively, if I already have a good understanding of a subject but feel that someone else in the meeting did not do an adequate job of explaining it, I will kindly expand upon their explanation with my own, ask everyone if they have understood it, and then explain that it is okay if they haven't because it would just be an indication that I have not explained it well enough (taking the blame upon myself). There are no stupid questions. Eliminating the embarrassment that others might feel can easily become addictive when you can see the positive results it brings and after you have had enough people thank you privately after a meeting has ended.

A Chief Technology Officer that I formerly worked with referred to the PMM and PM roles as the "spiders in the web". What he meant was that to some degree, those two roles are involved in every project, and coordinating the ever-important flow of information. This also means that we are often asking others for help to complete important tasks. As the PMM comes into contact with so many different roles (webmasters, UX designers, developers, PMs, etc.) it is important to foster those relationships. For example, giving credit where credit is due is not only the proper thing to do but also important in maintaining relationships with the people who assist you in completing important tasks. Being a good leader is about lifting up those around you. If you remember this as a PMM, the respect and trust that those people have for you will continue to grow. As a result, the amount and quality of information they bring you will increase and your deliverables will be that much better for it.

The Hybrid

Working closely with many different teams requires strong communication which is only possible if you speak the same language as everyone else. Unfortunately, this is easier said than done. Fortunately, it is also what sets a PMM apart from all of the other roles in your company.

The first thing to do is put your experience to good use. For example, do you come from a marketing background or education and already speak the same language as the marketing team? If so, start spending time with other teams to expand your horizons, learn their terminology, and see things through their eyes. Typically, the PMM reports to the Chief Marketing Officer or Vice President of Product Marketing (depending on the size of the organization) and belongs to the marketing team. However, it can be a useful practice to spend just three days a week with marketing and the other two days with other teams.

When it comes to working with different business units, a PMM should exist in three different worlds simultaneously:

- Marketing

- Product Management and Development

- Sales

Here are two examples of how the PMM can play a crucial role in working with these business units, seen from opposite points of view:

Marketing is often the most difficult for other business units to understand, due to its creative nature. This is especially true for developers who may find it difficult to grasp the Key Performance Indicators (KPIs) of the marketing team and how they organize their time and resources. This presents a golden opportunity for you, the PMM, to clarify marketing's role in the company to the other business units and make its activities and goals more transparent.

Many smaller companies have a Monday morning meeting as an opportunity for every team to highlight what it had accomplished during the previous week as well as what it would be focusing on during the upcoming week. Marketing generally highlights the latest blogs, newsletters, or other important information from its point of view.

After enough business lunches with the product and support teams, I knew that the presentations given by marketing during these meetings were not relatable to people outside of marketing. This was because there was no explanation of what the drive behind creating and marketing that material was, how the results were being measured, or how they affected sales. Therefore, whenever it was my turn to speak about what marketing was working on, I changed my approach to also explain why it should matter to everyone else.

During one such event, I only had two minutes to work with so I spent the first minute explaining the marketing team's KPIs, one of which included supplying our Sales team with sales leads. This was important to them because the more leads they got from us, the more sales they could potentially close. During the second minute, I used an example to explain that one way we went about collecting leads was to organize and host webinars. I then explained that for an upcoming webinar we were co-hosting with another organization, we had received over two-hundred registrations in just a few days but that only about thirty of those registrations were leads. "Does anyone know why all of the registrations are not leads?", I asked. No one (outside of a few people from the marketing team - but not all) raised their hands. The reason, I explained, was because a registrant must be both new to our database (in other words, not an existing customer or known prospect) and fit within our definition of Small and Medium Business, as that was the only segment we targeted. I then said that if everyone in our Sales team could share the information about the upcoming webinar in some form of social media, our opportunities for producing even more leads would vastly increase.

This may seem like a pretty simple approach but we should never assume that everyone is familiar with the way that other teams within their own organization operate (in fact, we should assume that they are not familiar with it). I received many positive responses for an easy speech that made the marketing team's work more visible and accessible.

On the flip side of that coin, the ultimate goal of spending time with PMs and developers is to have a deeper understanding of the product and be able to relay what you have learned to the marketing and sales teams. However, it is not sufficient to simply convey this information as the PMs would. One of the highly sought-after skills organizations are looking for in a PMM is the ability to understand products on a deeper technical level and then express what they have learned in human-understandable-speech for the other teams and rest of the world.

I have often invited developers to monthly meetings in which we spent at least one hour testing our products and Application Programming Interfaces (APIs). One time, my boss asked me what this had to do with marketing and why I would spend my time doing it. The product in question at that time was a security software that was installed on servers in a data center.

There were three main API calls in use during production: The first was to activate our product on the server, the second was to fetch a report that showed the result (success/failure) of our product and when it occurred (for auditing purposes), and the third was to capture the ongoing status of the product as it was performing its tasks. It was the third API call that interested me the most. This is because in all of our sales and marketing material, we emphasized our ability to automate the activation and reporting of this feature but no one had taken the time to speak to the developers and understand this third call.

A week later, our sales and marketing material reflected my new knowledge with mention of "automated real-time status checks" which immediately turned out to be a crucial selling point for the prospective clients who needed to know exactly when a service was being used and how much system resources it was consuming from their servers while it was active. My boss never questioned my use of time with our development team again and the rest of the marketing team was more than happy to have someone on-board who could identify these technical details that were otherwise lost in translation.

Another take-away from that example is that we cannot rely upon our development teams to understand what is valuable knowledge to prospects, sales, and marketing and then articulate it for us. For me, and for many PMMs I know, this is one of the most enjoyable parts of the role.

By understanding how different teams think, work, and speak, you can be the link among them. After all, the ultimate goal is to empower your sales and marketing teams with the knowledge and messaging that they need to create and nurture leads, and to win deals.

The next three chapters of this book look at how the PMM interacts with the business units of Marketing, Product Management and Development, and Sales, and how the highest level of impact can be achieved. It then ties all of that information together into a chapter dedicated to creating your unique positioning and messaging. Let's get started.

II

MARKETING

The PMM's Role within Marketing

Let's begin this chapter by explaining how product marketing is its own function within marketing. Depending on the size and focus of a company, the marketing team consists of many different roles. Here are some examples:

Content Marketers create and distribute material, such as blogs and videos, through social media to attract interest and generate leads, increase brand awareness, and engage with their online audience.

Digital/Online Marketers, Growth Hackers, and Demand Generation teams work with Search Engine Optimization, email marketing, ad campaigns, and other omni-channel approaches to reach an audience and grow the business. Sometimes, the audiences are already aware that they have a problem and require a solution. An example of this would be hosting a webinar to address an industry concern and then briefly pitching a specific product or company as the best available solution.

Business Intelligence may belong to a marketing team as it collects, stores, and analyzes data that can lead to strategic or operational changes.

Event Coordinators/Planners organize trade shows, conferences, and other events. This includes budgeting as well as planning and organizing venues, transportation, guest speakers, catering, and anything else relevant to that particular event.

Copywriters are responsible for writing content for various forms of marketing and advertising such as blogs, paid ads, and eBooks.

Graphic Designers are responsible for the creation and assembly of images, typography, illustrations, and other forms of visuals for both online and offline material such as websites, web banners, eBooks, brochures, and product sheets.

*Field Marketer*s are responsible for running marketing operations in their local markets and languages, including building local customer success stories.

While there are yet other roles to mention, it is only the PMM who focuses on the positioning of a product and the specific messaging created for delivering a Unique Selling Proposition (USP) by defining itself in the market and separating itself from competition as it drives both prospect and customer engagement. In addition, it is the PMM who works closely with

PMs and developers to plan and execute product releases and launches and to take detailed and often technical product information and turn it into key marketing and sales messages.

The PMM's cross-functional role keeps it constantly engaged with other business units and the tasks are quite often different than those of other roles within the marketing team. However, it is important to be plugged into the marketing team and aware of what its many different facets are working on. After all, the marketing team is the channel through which the PMM's positioning and messaging reaches the world.

Whether you are speaking about inbound or outbound marketing, the marketing team can greatly assist the PMM's search for the correct messaging. Be it visuals, copy, pricing explanations, or anything else that the PMM is involved in, the marketing team can help verify which methods work best and generate the most interest through A/B testing and other forms of validation and testing.

As an example of outbound marketing, understanding the success of the current product positioning with regard to demand generation is quite important. Is your message getting across to the market and driving awareness of your products? Is your positioning compelling and sufficiently self-explanatory to drive prospects to contact your company rather than just relying upon your sales team to cold call them?

As an example of inbound marketing, how many qualified leads has the marketing team provided to the global sales team so far this month? Last month? As part of the marketing team, the PMM is also responsible for these results and the team's achieved KPIs. For example, perhaps the sales team in Germany is receiving far fewer leads than the North American team. A visit or call to the German team might shed light on the product positioning and messaging and why it is currently less effective in Germany than in the USA. It could be that the German market responds more favorably to technical information while the USA is more concerned with the latest industry buzzwords. In this case, if you have positioned your products to appear simple and nontechnical, your products will receive less attention in Germany.

I remember seeing another PMM struggle with a similar issue. His team was developing a software application for Android and iOS devices that was picking up strongly in the USA. Unfortunately, the German market was far behind and as a result, his German sales team was making a conscious choice to sell other products in the portfolio and leave his behind so as to maximize the amount of commission they could generate for themselves.

He decided to take a trip to Germany to speak individually with members of the sales team as well as with a few customers. It turned out that the problem was a rather simple one: The German market loved the word "Automation". If a manual task could be automated, it justified the purchase of a product and yet, his messaging had not included this information. After a quick revision of his product marketing material to reflect how much manual work could be automated with the app as well as follow-up training to teach his sales team how to pitch it to their prospects, the sales in Germany skyrocketed.

Consistent Messaging

While various markets and verticals may require tweaked versions of the messaging as highlighted in the previous example, keeping the messaging as consistent as possible across all channels is the ultimate goal. The messages that you deliver about your product should be the same across sales decks, marketing and tutorial videos, eBooks, fact sheets, and other material as well as within the product itself.

Tone of voice also plays a major role in your company's branding and can be difficult to maintain consistently across the different communication channels. Agreeing with the marketing team and copywriter whether the tone of voice is serious or light-hearted is important. For example, is the tone of voice for the elevator pitch that you teach to your sales team the same as in the default sales presentation that you provide to them? Is it the same as the in-product messaging that you have written? How about external blogs or trade show booth design and messaging which is written or maintained by the marketing team? The PMM cannot do it all so agreeing upon a common tone of voice is important for everyone in your organization who creates externally communicated content.

Before content is published, look through it to ensure that the intended positioning and messaging have been captured correctly. Even though you may have written the original copy, there could have been a miscommunication during its creation or someone may have taken liberty to alter it when it landed on their desk.

I once wrote a two-sided fact sheet about a Windows application that my company developed and sold. One of the key selling points that I had identified was the ability for administrators to set and control the installation and configuration of the application across all of the computers in their network from just one central server. This was crucial for empowering the administrators while limiting the end-user options to ensure that the application was used in a standardized manner by every computer in the network.

As with all material at that company, it was handed over to our in-house copywriter for review and editing before publication. Luckily for me, I decided to quickly skim over it again after having received it back from the copywriter but before it had been publicly released. What I found in the new version was something akin to, "Administrators now have fewer options for configuration in the network!" The copywriter had clearly misunderstood the message and decided to "improve" it without consulting me. When I asked why this change had been made, the response was that it had been changed to be "more marketable".

Obviously, this is a humorous misunderstanding but if that fact sheet had been sent to potential customers who also received a link to a tutorial video which had the opposite messaging, it would have led to confusion and ultimately, lack of confidence in the company and its products. Regardless of the material produced by the marketing team, make sure that you have the first and final word in the product messaging and that it is clear and consistent across all material.

Utilizing two rounds of review is quite typical. The first round is for you to sign off on what the copywriter or owner of the material has written and the second round is so that you can see how the copy looks after it has been placed within the document's design. Sometimes the messaging sounds and looks good when written as plain text but when inserted into a specific design or format, it may become apparent that it still requires tweaking. As long as this review process is agreed upon with both the copywriter and graphic designer, there will be no issues when/if you ask to change something that you already approved. As an example, perhaps your copy ends with the sentence, "Product Y delivers a Return On Investment of X% and is the right solution for you!" but now that you have seen how it looks in the final design, that last sentence makes the entire copy too long and should be removed. You may ask the designer to delete it, and instead, place a star icon elsewhere on the document with the new and minimal copy of "X% ROI", thus conveying your message and producing the best possible visual.

In another example of consistent messaging, if your company outsources the drafting of white papers to an external agency, that agency will need assistance with your sales pitch and USP. They will receive product and feature facts from your PMs and will generate their own sources for statistics and industry trends but it is imperative that the PMM be involved in keeping the overall messaging consistent with your company's marketing material.

It is typical that a PMM team will generate product positioning and messaging on a global level which will then be filtered down to field marketing in other regions or countries for localization. Working with the field marketers to maintain consistency is important so that they don't stray too far from the intended message or communication style.

At a large company where I formerly worked, the PMM team was located at the headquarters, defined the messaging, and then conveyed it to the field marketers in eighteen countries. It was understood that the message may change a bit and different buzzwords may be used to better appeal to the different markets. In addition, each country would reach out to its customer base and produce its own local customer success stories / case studies to enforce the sales message. The success stories were created by using templates, instructions, and guidelines that were maintained by the centralized PMM team to ensure consistency. However, this was possible only because each country had the resources to handle the translations, success story creation, and material design on its own. Each time a new success story was created, it was sent to headquarters for review and approval before publication.

In a smaller company I worked with, everything had to be created and processed at headquarters because the smaller offices in other countries consisted only of sales and support teams and did not possess the resources required to generate their own success stories. In this type of situation, it is important to convince the entire company of the messaging that you developed so that they do not request alternative versions in which each country wants its own version of the same material. Agreeing to create several versions of even a single document can quickly become a considerable strain on both the PMM and graphic designer as each version will require updating whenever a single change or update is required. However, when translating material from one language to another, it is entirely acceptable for the translations to stray a bit. For example, if a buzzword works better in one country than in another, it can be swapped out in the translated version so long as the translation company (or internal resources that are used to translate) keeps a database of it for future reference and use.

Success Stories / Case Studies

After years of interviewing customers, it has become apparent to me that success stories (or case studies) are one of the key elements that prospects access when considering your product. What they want to know is how the product has helped other people or companies that are similar to them. They are looking for assurance that they will experience similar results.

Likewise, if I had to list the one item most requested by sales teams I have worked with over the years, customer success stories would be it.

When creating success stories, highlight the following elements:

1. The customer's background

2. The challenges and pain points the customer was experiencing before finding your product

3. Why the customer specifically chose your product

4. What the results and impact were to the customer's business

The goal is for others to identify with the company and its problems and then imagine their business experiencing similar satisfaction with your product.

Visiting Customers and Prospects

Working in marketing can often be challenging as we are constantly striving to produce updated and catchy content which our Sales team can use when selling products and services. However, I can testify to having very quickly fallen out of touch with the day-to-day challenges and obstacles that sales teams face simply because I was not on the frontline with them. As PMMs, we need to put ourselves on the front-line of communication with both prospects and customers and alongside our sales teams.

At one company, I kept up to date by traveling with a particular salesperson for a series of prospect and customer visits at least once every two months. This salesperson would book three days of travel with six visits per day. It was a tough schedule but ensured that I would sit in front of both existing customers (satisfied and unsatisfied ones) as well as people who had not yet purchased our products.

Customers would chat with the salesperson and explain how life with our products had been working for them. Inevitably, the discussion almost always turned to two topics: Pricing and product roadmaps. I paid close attention to their struggles with bugs in our software and their interest in any upcoming features we were developing. This was my time to shine. Regardless of whether my salesperson had been paying attention to our internal company communication about roadmap updates, he always deferred to me as I had the best product and roadmap knowledge from working so closely with the PMs, developers, and marketing teams. Working within marketing also meant that I was familiar with the dates of upcoming eBooks, webinars, and other items that the customer might find interesting or relevant to his or her business.

Happy with your product or not, customers will often ask about a functionality which you do not currently provide. If you convey this inquiry to your PMs and development team, it may have the potential to become a new feature or even a new product. The best example of this that I remember was when the German Country Manager of a company I worked for visited one of the largest software companies in Germany. They asked him if our software could support entire virtual drives, also known as Logical Unit Numbers, as opposed to individual magnetic disks or Solid State Drives. Their concern was that targeting every individual physical drive in a Storage Area Network took too long. If they could target large virtual drives, which are made up of many individual physical drives, they would vastly speed up the use of our software.

Our Country Manager brought the question to our product team which decided that it made sense to build this functionality. Not only did they add support for virtual drives in our product but we spun it off as its own new and altogether separate product which our Country Manager sold at an extraordinary price. It opened doors to countless other prospects who could utilize the same functionality. Consequently, our sales increased and I created new material to highlight this new product.

Visiting prospects has also provided me with priceless insights. You never know which way the discussion will go and no matter how much you prepare or how much product and marketing knowledge you have, there is always at least one question which you will not know the answer to. While there is nothing wrong with not knowing the answer, the worst thing you can do is improvise an answer that may be incorrect. Make sure that they see you write it down and then follow up with an email or phone call later after you have spoken to your colleagues and determined the correct answer.

First, when visiting someone who has not previously heard your sales pitch, your salesperson should give a basic presentation about who you are, what products or services you provide, and how they solve the pain points that the prospect is experiencing. Does the information do a proper job in a short and concise way or do the prospects have initial questions that your material should have done a better job explaining? Additionally, do the prospects gain a quick understanding of why they should ask for a demo and continue down the buyer's journey or do they have objections which you should have been able to address and overcome already in the opening sales pitch?

Asking your salesperson for permission for you to give this opening speech can be quite eye-opening and vastly different than simply listening to someone else deliver it. You may notice that as you proceed through the presentation, all of the relevant material is there but the order in which it is presented doesn't feel right when compared to how you and your colleagues in marketing envisioned it. Alternatively, the presentation may be missing messages or information deemed important by the marketing or product teams but has, for one reason or another, not been included.

I once visited a prospect with a salesperson only to discover that one of the slides used in the presentation was seven years old. It was a slide that showed all of the endorsements that our products had obtained over the years and yet, it was so old that most, but not all, of the endorsements were no longer valid. After the meeting, I asked why our newly updated endorsements slide had not been used and received two answers: First, the salesperson had no idea where to find the latest slides (we will address this in the "Sales" chapter) and second, the updated slide did not contain the old, and yet still valid, endorsements which had been deemed outdated by the marketing team and were therefore excluded from the updated slide. One of those old endorsements in particular was still important for the sales vertical that this salesperson worked with, which is why he still used the old slide. It was a powerful lesson that tagging along with salespeople is the best way to understand their daily struggles and use of your material.

Equally important is whether or not your material sells itself without a trained salesperson explaining it. That same salesperson and I once visited a manager who had the decision-making and purchasing power within his company. After introductions, the manager began to speak about the summer cabin he was building. My salesperson seemed fascinated by this story and prompted him with questions which furthered the discussion. Before I knew it, fifty-five minutes had passed and we only had five minutes left before we had to run to the taxi and arrive at our next meeting on time. As we were excusing ourselves and rushing out the door, my salesperson handed a folder of our marketing and sales material to the prospect who promised to read it. Once in the taxi, I remarked how little chance I thought we had at signing that company as a new customer since we had not spoken at all about our products. My salesperson assured me that building a relationship with the manager was much more important in that particular situation than presenting our normal sales pitch and that if he read the material, our products would speak for themselves and meet his needs. A month later, he was our customer and two months after that, he agreed to be the subject of one of our success stories.

Each piece of material should be able to stand on its own and communicate the USP of your product offering. This means that a prospect does not need to read four separate pieces of sales collateral to understand the full picture but can drop in at any point in the buyer's journey, read the one piece of material that they have come into contact with or deem important at that point in time, and see the value in choosing your product. This can be achieved through storytelling. An example story which could be applied equally to a sales deck, product sheet, blog, case study, and eBook is seen here:

1. Background of the situation

2. Identified problem

3. Solution

4. Results

Attending Trade Shows

Visualize the opportunity to speak with numerous prospects on the same day. Trade shows are wonderful opportunities for a company to promote its brand, connect with customers, pitch to prospects, keep an eye on competitors, and immerse itself in the latest market trends. They also provide a useful opportunity for the PMM to test out the latest material and messaging in person.

While booth design is handled by graphic designers, it is the PMM who decides what messaging it contains. Does it speak clearly to the audience by explaining in just a few words what it is that you have to offer the event's attendees?

Do the brochures and other handouts emphasize and align with your main message? Imagine that everyone in your booth is engaged in conversation and someone approaches and picks up sales material to read on their own, does it speak for itself and convince them to stay for an opportunity to speak with you or one of your colleagues? Attending trade shows and attempting to pitch your offering to someone who has never heard of you or your company is a test not only of your messaging but of your ability to articulate it.

Additionally, does your company have the opportunity to register for one of the speaker slots? If so, volunteer yourself! There is no better way to measure your messaging prowess than by winning over a crowd of complete strangers through the use of a few slides, stories, and product explanations.

Another useful exercise is to interview customers and prospects who visit your booth as well as strangers walking throughout the event. This can lead to market and industry insights and trends or even help you improve your own positioning and messaging. For example, if you interview someone who has just left your booth or the booth of one of your competitors, that person will use their own words to describe what it is that they understand your products (and those of your competitor) do, leading to a new and fresh way of marketing your product.

Prospects may provide the most useful insights as they have not yet heard your product messaging. Ask them why they chose to attend that particular event and what products and solutions they are looking for.

Interviewing people who have not approached your booth can greatly assist you with understanding what people are expecting from that event in general. This may help you in better positioning your company for other future events in the same industry. Imagine that seven out of ten people you interview claim to be searching for an "omni-channel solution". This may describe a new product you recently launched and now with this knowledge, you want to include those exact words into the booth design of your next event to ensure that you do not miss any opportunities as people walk by.

Internal Company Events

In addition to external events, the marketing team is usually responsible for planning and organizing internal company events. While the logistics are handled by others, the PMM is usually involved in planning the content of the event.

During the planning of an annual company event, someone in my marketing team suggested a "Product Obstacle Course". In several rooms of our office, we built small labs for each of our products. Employees from all of the business units were divided into mixed groups which would navigate from room to room, completing product-related tasks in each before moving on to the next. It was a great method for face-to-face training and collecting feedback as well as listening to their discussions and experiences. The PMs especially profited from this activity as people who would not normally provide feedback or even test the products were more keen to explain what they did or did not understand or like about the products.

As I was still inexperienced at the time of this exercise, I learned that I had been focusing too narrowly on relaying product knowledge and that this had caused me to miss a wonderful opportunity to put the right product messaging in the thoughts of every participant as they moved from obstacle to obstacle. What better way to ensure that everyone in your company can deliver the same elevator pitch about each of your products before they are were permitted to move on to the next obstacle!

Later, at another company, I hosted a quarterly "Sales Academy" session for all recruits new to the sales and marketing teams as well as external partners who were required to pay to attend. We sold solutions, rather than products. That meant that we focused on identifying the prospects' problems and then solving them, rather than promoting or selling specific products.

Throughout this week-long Sales Academy event, each PMM would present the solutions that they worked most closely with. While we demonstrated the solutions and showed screenshots during our presentations, we focused on highlighting the values and benefits that they offered as opposed to explaining how the actual products worked or what features they contained. In order to avoid smothering the students with too many slides and presentations, we included as much interaction as possible. This took many forms including group presentations and students pairing off and taking turns selling to one another.

At the end of the week, the students were assigned to teams that were required to pass an exam consisting of two steps: First, each group met with a mock prospect (two teachers) to use the knowledge they had gained throughout the week to sell the solutions and ensure a second meeting. The second meeting was one-on-one between a student and a teacher; the student would act as a consultant and demonstrate the solutions to the teacher.

After the week, the students would go back to their different countries and offices and begin their actual work. We knew that everyone who had successfully completed the Sales Academy had at least a basic understanding of our solutions and positioning in the market. Later, PMs provided them with specific solution information that enforced our training.

Analyst Relations

When developing your positioning, messaging, and USP, working with third party analysts and research organizations to assess your company and its products can be an invaluable asset. Analyst relations is a challenging and time-consuming task that can often fall to the PMM. Having your company assessed and then ranked alongside its competitors can be an extremely strong sales tool if the analyst's results are favorable. Simply pointing to positive results from a well-respected third party, and saying, "Here you can see that we are one of the front-runners in our field" is sometimes enough to win the deal with a prospect who is already convinced that your product is necessary and simply needs to select a company to provide it. Additionally, paying a market research company to write a report on the advantages of your products can be a useful sales tool that highlights the ROI experienced by your customers.

While this can produce great results, the time needed to provide information to these external companies, meeting with them both in person and virtually, and budgeting for their services, is extremely time-consuming. In larger organizations, it is possible to dedicate a person to oversee this important task while in smaller organizations, you as the PMM may need to juggle it along with other tasks. If this is your situation, sharing the responsibility with colleagues is a good option so that you are plugged into the external content that is created to highlight your company's strengths and to also give you enough time to focus on your core responsibilities.

Keep in mind that your relationship with the analyst will have an impact on the outcome of the results. Maintaining consistent and professional communication and being able to answer technical and product-related questions is favorable for both you and the analyst and proves that your company takes the study seriously. As always, communication is key. Building a healthy working relationship with the analyst will be to everyone's benefit.

Once, when the latest analyst results were published, my company was ranked second best in the world. Although this was an excellent outcome, our top management was unhappy because they expected us to be listed as first. They requested a call with the analyst to discuss the already public results. During the call, our management team expressed their dismay and annoyance with the results and blamed the analyst for not properly understanding the industry. Not only was this embarrassing to listen to, but it seemed to me that they had forgotten that exactly one year from then we would be receiving the next year's results from the same analyst. Would attacking this person really foster a good relationship? Luckily, we had a very professional PMM on our team who was able to repair the damage and work with the analyst for years to come. Yet again, good communication and healthy relationships prevailed.

Let's now take a look at how the PMM works with PMs and development, and where the product information originates, before it makes its way to marketing.

III

PRODUCT MANAGEMENT
AND DEVELOPMENT

I have witnessed and experienced first-hand how the PM and PMM roles work in tandem and sometimes overlap. The smaller the company, the more overlap of responsibilities and tasks, while the larger the company, the less overlap. The PM works closely with the development teams and focuses on documenting product requirements, prioritizing the roadmap, and meeting the release deadlines. The PMM on the other hand, focuses on market research and strategy, externally communicated content, messaging, and positioning.

Without a clearly defined PMM role in the organization, it is quite common that the marketing team does not have a strong understanding of the product and is often late in receiving news about upcoming product launches and features. The best way for a PMM to affect the success of a product and to support the marketing team is to get involved in the development process from the very beginning of the product lifecycle.

Here is a typical way of defining the product lifecycle:

1. Conception
2. Development - Including an Alpha version, Beta version, and Release Candidate
3. Product Launch
4. Growth
5. Maturity
6. Decline
7. Withdrawal

It happens all too often that a marketing team will catch wind of a new product or feature launch somewhere around the Beta version. As you can imagine, this can oftentimes be rather frustrating as the late notice may not leave much time for material creation or positioning the upcoming launch into an already planned campaign or event. The PMM can solve this problem by plugging into the product lifecycle from the very beginning. In fact, the conceptualized product or feature could have its product messaging or press release already written by the PMM before the development even begins. Additionally, what if your messaging focuses on meeting the requirements of your clients rather than simply listing the features included in the proposed end result? What more could a marketing team ask of a person than the delivery of that information to them on a silver platter months before the initial launch?

On one occasion, my company had created a Windows application for connecting, identifying, and servicing up to ten iOS (iPhones and iPads) and Android devices. In practice, it was used by refurbishing companies to connect devices to just one computer running our software and to deploy a diagnostics check simultaneously on all of them. This was an integral part of the reverse supply chain in which devices would be returned to the Point of Sale for one reason or another (usually broken or returned for a discount on a new device) and the receiving warehouses could process them in large batches.

After a few years of satisfactory success, the overwhelming feedback from our customers was that ten devices at a time was not sufficient and required too much manual work when the Android device drivers were not automatically recognized by the Windows operating system.

The CEO asked me to write a sales pitch for the ideal product that would meet and exceed the needs of our prospects and customers. The messaging I wrote highlighted how easy the product was to use, how hundreds of devices could be processed within an eight-hour work day on just one computer, and how every processed device would generate its own detailed report for auditing purposes. Shortly after, the CEO commissioned a new development team to begin creating this dream product and for the next twelve months, I would drop in to visit and remind them of the product messaging and sales pitch on which the entire project was based.

What they built was our very own Linux-based operating system that did not have identification issues with Android devices (also Linux-based) and therefore allowed a user to connect and process up to fifty devices (both iOS and Android) at once and send the results in real-time to our Cloud for reporting purposes. Once in the Cloud, the reports could be automatically exported via an API call into the customer's ERP system for continued processing as they went through additional stages, such as physical repair, in the warehouse.

The final product our developers came up with was nothing short of spectacular; the original messaging had been used to create sales and marketing material well before the launch, the sales team had been properly trained, and our sales results were stunning.

Development Methodology and Tools

Relying on PMs to inform you when major and minor releases are planned is important teamwork but being plugged into the development process yourself provides yet another level of much needed visibility. What methodology (if any) is your development team using? Scrum? Kanban? Waterfall? Something else? Nothing at all? How do they organize their work?

If a certain methodology is followed, it is relatively simple to jump onboard where applicable. For example, if your team has daily stand-up sessions in the mornings, get yourself invited. This will give you insight as to what features/bug fixes are being addressed and whether or not the schedule is on track. Better yet, attend the planning sessions so that you are aware of, or can even affect, which features have been included in the next development cycle.

After you are familiar with how the development team operates, work with the PMs to have them share the information with you in a more official manner. I often find that while I do not have enough time to join the more detailed development meetings, a short weekly or bi-weekly meeting with the PMs provides me with quick and straightforward updates on what to expect and when, as well as any changes since our last meeting. How much time you spend with the PMs and/or developers really depends upon the size and practices of your company. Ultimately, what matters is that you receive the information you need and in a way that allows you to most efficiently turn it around into marketing and sales material.

If you are fortunate, both the marketing and development teams will use the same tools for tracking their backlogs, ongoing projects, approvals, etc. However, this is rarely the case. Either way, you should have access to whatever tools both teams use to ensure you are receiving consistent information.

After you have access to the ticket tracking tool(s) used by the development team, it is wise to watch the larger tickets which encompass many smaller tickets and dependencies. This will provide you with visibility over the status of larger features and releases. Additionally, the PMs can alert you to important tickets to keep your eye on. These tickets offer you the perfect platform to affect the outcome and visibility of the development efforts.

As an example, a development team I worked with had decided to give our clients the option to integrate one of our products with a popular social media app. As this added functionality was only compatible with one of our five products, the PM had decided to market it only to the clients who used that particular product. The plan was to display a banner inside of our central Management Console which would only be visible to the users of this one product to inform them that this new functionality was available. When I reviewed the development ticket for this project, I saw a mock-up of the banner and it was immediately clear to me that we could leverage the new functionality to entice clients who were using our other products to adopt this one as well.

I added my comments to the ticket and requested that the UX designers working in that team revise the banner, and display it to all of our customers, regardless of which products they had. I wrote the new text to be included in the banner and explained the reasoning for using this release as an opportunity to not only update the users of this product but to upsell it to all of our other customers who did not have it. The PM was happy with the suggestion and the scope of the release was changed.

This is also a perfect example for why the PMM should be involved during the planning phase before development has begun. The entire scope of the release could have been agreed upon from the beginning, rather than changed halfway through.

Product Launches

Defining product release steps with PMs is a valuable way to ensure that all tasks and responsibilities are clear to both parties for a successful launch. This plan can be thought of as a "Product Release Plan" or a "Product Marketing Release Plan" and can apply to both minor and major version releases.

Some companies define a separate release plan for each type of release. For example, there could be four types of releases: Priority 1 (P1), P2, P3, and P4. A P1 release plan would contain more steps than a P2, which would contain more than a P3, which would contain more than a P4. This is because a P1 release would make a bigger impact on the customers and market and would therefore require more work and deliverables from the company in its promotion than a smaller release such as a P4.

However, P4 should not be overlooked or thought of as unimportant. Letting your clients know what changes have been made on a detailed level is important so that they don't miss new and useful functionality. Oftentimes in Business-to-Business, the client's IT or development teams play an important role in influencing their decision-makers to continue using your products. The PMM should not forget these important stakeholders; making a changelog available and relevant to them is a strong marketing tool.

Here is an example P2 release plan:

Weeks prior to launch	Responsible person	Actions	Product status
8	PM	Invite a few customers to test the new product or feature as Beta	Beta
6	PM	1. Communicate the intended launch date to the PMM 2. Provide the PMM with a list of Beta customers and specify two or three which would make good customer success stories	Beta
6	PMM	Reach out to the chosen customer and begin creating the success story	Beta
4	PM + PMM	Develop a training package for all relevant business units	Release Candidate
4	PMM	Work with the Marketing team to update all relevant sales & marketing material (including localization) • Sales deck slide (new or update) • Product sheet update • Website update • Customer success story • Blog, eBook, webinar, or video	Release Candidate
3	PM	Update all relevant Technical Support material • Support articles • User manuals	Release Candidate
2	PM + PMM	Deliver training to all relevant business units	Ready for Launch
2	PM	Deliver the internal Changelog to the PMM	Ready for Launch
2	PMM	Use the Changelog to create the messaging used to market the launch • In-product message • Email to customers	Ready for Launch
0	PM + PMM	Launch	Launch

While this is an example P4 plan:

Weeks prior to launch	Responsible person	Actions	Product status
2	PM	Communicate the intended launch date to PMM	Ready for Launch
2	PM	Deliver the internal Changelog to the PMM	Ready for Launch
1	PMM	Use the Changelog to create the messaging used to market the launch • In-product message	Ready for Launch
0	PM + PMM	Launch	Launch

Defining the deliverables required by each of the different release plans is a good way to maintain consistency and a high level overview of what is expected. Here is an example of the required deliverables for each type of release:

	P1	P2	P3	P4
In-product message	x	x	x	x
Email to customers	x	x	x	
Sales deck slide (new or update)	x	x	x	
Product sheet update	x	x		
Website update	x	x		
Customer success story	x	x		
Blog, eBook, webinar, or video	x			
Press release	x			

It is important to follow a product release plan to align the development, marketing, and sales teams for each release so that the new product or feature and its sales collateral and messaging will be available for a smooth delivery on the expected launch date.

The KPIs for PMs and development teams usually revolve around product releases which means that when the product is technically ready for shipping in time for the defined deadline, they will have met their goal. However, if the marketing team is busy with another overlapping launch, event, or project, it could hold the development team back from achieving their intended public launch date. Additionally, the sales team may be aware that the product is technically ready for launch but without the proper training or sales collateral, they cannot begin to sell it and meet their own increasing sales targets. Some companies combat this issue by making the new product or feature available to the customer base but not advertising or promoting it until the marketing team and launch are ready.

On the flip side, it happens all too often that PMs and the development team do not meet their release deadlines due to unforeseen technical or resource problems. To avoid marketing the launch of a product or release that has become delayed, some organizations intentionally stagger the product marketing releases behind the expected release dates. For example, if the PMM agrees with the PMs that each product marketing launch will be scheduled for exactly four weeks after the intended launch date communicated by the PMs and outlined in the product roadmap, there is enough of a buffer that if delays occur, they are automatically accounted for, and even expected, in the process.

Product-Focused Campaigns

As your marketing team plans and executes campaigns throughout the year, the PMM plays an important role by tying in product releases. If a campaign revolves around a major product release, the PMM may be in charge of leading the campaign. In this case, work together with the members of your marketing team who are in charge of other types of campaigns to create common guidelines. Here are a few considerations:

- What are the start-and-end dates of the campaign?

- Who is the target audience?

- What are the objectives? This includes marketing objectives such as the projected number of leads obtained but also sales objectives, such as how much profit will be generated as a result of the campaign or how many new customers it will bring in.

- What is the defined messaging for customers and prospects and the positioning for the market in general?

- What are the milestones and deliverables of the campaign from beginning to end and who in the team is responsible for them?

- Who must approve each deliverable before it can be marked as "Done"?

- What are the dependencies tied to the different deliverables?

- What are the defined promotional activities?

- How is the campaign communicated to other business units within your organization and what input is required of them to help further its success (such as sharing the news in social media)?

By documenting everything and keeping every stakeholder up to date from the very beginning, a PMM can ensure a successful product campaign.

Product Roadmaps

To begin planning the launch of a new product or feature, the PMs need to have roadmaps in place that tell you what is coming and when. The roadmaps are the result of the PM's and other stakeholders' prioritization of bug fixes and new features and products. It is the PM's job to make these roadmaps visible to the different business units within the organization.

What about the customers? The PMM has the ability to make the customers feel like part of the family by including them in this process. An always tricky question is whether or not you can release your roadmaps externally. While the external versions will surely not be as detailed as the internal ones, they can still give your customers visibility as to the direction you are taking your product and be a useful tool in making your customers feel like they can provide feedback and affect the course of development. However, it can also be a risky game in case plans change and what you have previously communicated is no longer true.

Additionally, be wary of making external roadmaps available to prospects as they may sometimes use it as an excuse to delay purchase. This was a lesson that I learned the hard way during a visit to a prospect with one of my salespeople. When the prospect asked about a certain functionality, I proudly declared that it was already in our roadmap and that we would support it within the next six months. The answer I received was, "I like your product but will wait to buy from you until you support that feature." The salesperson was not happy with how things had gone and taught me a valuable lesson that many times prospects will ask for features or functionality that they won't even use once they have it. Instead, they search for any functionality that you do not currently support as a way to procrastinate or avoid the purchasing decision.

It was that salesperson's style to avoid speaking about what was to come. Instead, he identified the client's current pain points and then sold them our readily available solution to meet their immediate needs. It became irrelevant that a certain feature would become available in half a year. That would come when it came and by that point they would be already happily using our product and the additional feature would only increase their loyalty to our company.

Technical Support and User Groups

The PM knows best when it comes to prioritizing which features and bug fixes will be included in the next release. It is important for the PMM to understand this prioritization, as well as how and why the roadmap has been constructed this way. A good place to begin is the source from which the PMs receive their information. Do they travel frequently to visit customers and collect feedback? Do they organize their own user group sessions which consist of the most influential customers? Do they have regular calls scheduled with the highest paying customers?

Another important source of product-related feedback that makes its way to the PM and which should not be forgotten is the technical support team.

Once, the most respected developer in our team was giving a presentation to the rest of the development team, the PMs, and me. All of the other developers looked up to him and he later went on to become the Chief Technology Officer. During this particular speech, he was addressing an issue that had been plaguing the development team for the past year. There were five different products and the development team was split into five smaller teams to evenly account for each product; there was so much extended functionality and configuration options related to all five products that it had become impossible for any one person in the development team to know everything.

To address this, he had a very simple solution: "When in doubt, ask the technical support team." He went on to explain that while the developers tend to keep their heads down and focus on their own products and issues, the technical support team came into contact with customers every single day to answer questions and resolve problems for every product that we sold. He then asked a difficult product-related question. When no one offered an immediate reply, he said that he had asked the same question of the technical support team the day before and had not only received a wonderful and accurate answer but was told that they had been asked that same question by customers three times the previous week.

Because of the level of contact that the technical support team has with customers and the number of detailed questions and issues they face, they are also a frequent source of feature requests and the voice of customer demand. It is therefore in the best interest of the PMM to know how the technical support team communicates this information to the PMs for escalation to the development team. Do they write tickets in an internal system that must be justified with business value (the number of customers requesting a particular feature, the amount of money that each customer pays to the organization, etc.) and then approved by the PMs before submitted into the development team's backlog?

Understanding and plugging into this flow of information is a foolproof method for understanding what customers are after and why. From the PMM's point of view, it is a method for free and easily available market research. For example, a customer may ask for a technical feature to be implemented but what is the reason behind their request? What is the customer trying to accomplish and what words did they use to describe that need? Perhaps what they are asking for is already available but they just aren't aware of it. This could be an indication that the product information they have received is not clear enough or communicated in the correct way.

User groups are another great way to incorporate client feedback into the development process. It may fall upon the PM to organize them but the PMM can also be involved. By gathering together your most important and influential customers on a regular basis, you can share with them the external roadmaps and ask for their feedback. Do they agree on the direction you are going? Do they prefer to see something else? Oftentimes, it is clients who provide you with the next brilliant step in evolving your products, and for the PMM, the clients may also provide you with the right words to use in your product messaging. For example, perhaps you market a product powered by "machine learning" but your biggest client refers to it as "artificial intelligence". If it is true and resonates better within your market and with similar customers, why not switch wording?

In-Product Marketing

While marketing and sales material are great for attracting prospects and upselling to existing customers, in-product marketing is a wonderfully effective method for upselling.

My very first lesson about in-product marketing came while working at a company that centered all of its products around a central admin tool. This admin tool was responsible for storing licenses and usage logs for every one of the products installed on client machines which would call the admin tool to consume a license and generate a log whenever they were used. At one point, two PMs and I were on tour in the USA, visiting our largest customers. During one of these visits, I witnessed a user navigate to the Licenses & Logs page. What she saw on this page was a tab for each of our different products. When she clicked on the first tab (product), I saw that she had copious amounts of licenses remaining and had generated thousands of logs in the past month. However, when she clicked on any other tab, she was confronted with a blank space where the license and log information should be. These tabs contained no information because her company had not purchased or used any of these products.

What I saw here was a golden opportunity to sell the unpurchased products to her and our other customers. After the tour was over, I sat down for a chat with our Director of Research & Development and agreed that marketing those products inside of our admin tool could lead to increased sales. Together, we created a mock-up, which our UX team later implemented, in which each tab of unpurchased product would now include a brief description of the product, a link to a tutorial video, and a link to the product's page on our website. Suddenly, we had a centralized admin tool that also marketed and sold all of our other products to existing clients. As a result, sales increased and we kept vigilant for other opportunities like this.

Development teams may also turn to the PMM to write and approve in-product instructions and tips; i.e., the best way to word a phrase or sentence within the product itself to make it as self-explanatory as possible. This can be a slippery slope that consumes more and more of your time. While you can play a large role in supplying the best in-product copy and instructions, it is better to work alongside other stakeholders such as the PMs or a technical writer who can spend more of their time handling the details so that you do not become derailed from your priorities.

Instead of doing it all yourself, partner with the PMs or technical writers to ensure that the same terminology used in the marketing and sales collateral is also used in the products themselves. This also applies to user manuals, online technical support articles, and other types of technical instructions and content. The actual writing of this content may be handled by other people in the organization but the PMM can make sure that what is written aligns with the same terminology that is used elsewhere. For example, are the products referred to as "Products" or "Solutions" on the website as well as in an offline user manual? Are the names of certain features the same in both a public white paper as well as within the product itself?

Too many companies do not use the same wording in their externally shared material as in their products. Not only is it confusing for the customers and prospects but for the company as well. The larger the company, the more difficult it is to remain in sync with what each team is working on.

IV

SALES

Sales Team Structure and Goals

With all of the information that you collect and process from the technical world, it comes down to the marketing and sales teams to convey it. You, the PMM, are responsible for empowering those teams to sell your products, prevail over competition, and deliver your USP with ease. Empowering the sales teams with the proper training, tools, and processes to achieve their sales targets is a huge part of the PMM role and is often referred to as "Sales Enablement".

Understanding how your sales team is structured and their goals is a good place to begin. First, what does the team hierarchy look like? Who are the managers, how many of them are there, where are they located, and what are their responsibilities? This will help you identify your main contacts within the team. Managers can act as the voice of the team when you need to collect feedback on how well your messaging, positioning, sales collateral, or other activities are being received. Additionally, they can help convey the latest updates and news to their teams and enforce mandatory activities such as any training that you have prepared.

What about those who are not managers? Are they separated into hunters (those who search for new customers) and farmers (those who provide account management and upselling to existing customers) or do they perform both of these responsibilities?

What are the defined sales verticals within their teams? One common type of sales vertical is geographic location. At a smaller-sized company I was familiar with, there was one dedicated salesperson for Germany, one for Austria, and one for Switzerland while at a larger-sized company, the entire German speaking team was free to sell in any and all of those three countries. Likewise, your company may place no virtual boundaries over the entire USA or have a structure in which each salesperson is responsible for a specific geographic region.

In addition to geographic and language borders, are the salespeople separated into industry verticals? What are they? Examples include pharmaceutical, automotive, and information technology. This is important when forming your value proposition as different verticals respond better to specific messaging, pain points, and terminology.

Besides sales verticals, keep up to date on sales targets and results. This information may be more easily accessible in smaller organizations than in larger ones but it is important to know the goals of the sales team as well as how much they have achieved in any particular month, quarter, or year. These sales targets are not just important for the individual salespeople, but are often the shared KPIs for other business units within the organization. Many people in your company may not be directly selling the products themselves but are nonetheless striving for the best possible results to ensure that they will receive their quarterly or yearly bonuses.

As the PMM, do you have visibility as to which products are selling better than others? This can strongly influence your strategy in case the positioning, messaging, sales collateral, and internal training of certain products requires more attention. As you focus to increase product adoption, you will be increasing product revenue and directly affecting the sales results.

Access to the company's Customer Relationship Management (CRM) tool can be useful in keeping an eye on the pipeline. A PMM I used to work with set up a system within our CRM so that he would receive an automatic email notification whenever a salesperson changed a prospect's status in the buyer's journey. For example, if a salesperson moved a prospect's sales status from 10% to 20%, it indicated that the prospect had progressed beyond simple awareness into genuine interest. The PMM then followed up with the salesperson directly to ask if any additional support was needed to finalize the sale of the product. Depending on the size of your sales team, this may be overkill but visibility is important and CRM systems can make it happen.

Training

After you are up to speed and aligned with the operation of the sales team, it is time to begin planning your sales enablement activities, which usually center around training. Depending upon the company that you work for, product training for the sales team may be hosted by PMs, PMMs, or a combination of both.

At one of my previous companies, the PMs were focused on their backlogs, bug fixes, and upcoming features and were not so directly involved with the sales teams. When it came time to deliver training on the latest product information, the PMs simply sent the latest information to the PMMs who then identified the relevant information for sales, created slide decks and videos, and used that material to host training sessions.

However, it can also be that the PMs take more responsibility and deliver training themselves. In this scenario, the best value that the PMM can add is to either act as a consultant to the PM in making sure that the training material is relevant and memorable to the sales team or to deliver their own complementary training sessions along with the PM's sessions. I experienced this quite a few times when a PM explained how a product works and then a PMM explained why it is important to our prospects.

PMs usually spend almost all of their time focusing on their products and sometimes find it hard to swim back up from the technical details to the surface level. As with any training or trainer, it is easy to weigh the material down with too much text, too much detailed information, and worst of all, messages that are not relevant or interesting to the audience. The PMM can serve as the solution to this problem by putting himself or herself in both the salesperson's and customer's shoes and helping to shape the training material to reflect what really needs to be conveyed. Some examples of this are the following:

- Why should the salespeople care about this training? How will it help increase their performance?

- What is the entertainment approach to the training

which makes the information interesting and memorable?

- What will be stimulating enough to make the salespeople want to relay what they have learned to their customers and prospects?

- What is the call to action at the end of the training? Is there an activity the salespeople should complete or a new sales goal that has been set for them?

- What is the follow-up to the training that enforces the message, and ensures that it remains in the salespeople's long-term memory?

When you create value for the sales team and convince them of the benefits of their products, they will see new avenues for meeting their sales targets and will, in turn, pass those values and benefits on to their prospects.

So how should training be delivered? Face-to-face training is always optimal but may not be possible if you have offices in many locations and countries. Additionally, face-to-face may not be scalable if it requires you to constantly travel from office to office, never leaving you with enough time to focus on your other tasks.

Learning Management System

A great way to organize training for all business units within an organization is through the use of a Learning Management System (LMS). An LMS is a platform that allows you to create courses and exams, upload files such as presentations and video recordings, and distribute certifications, badges, and other rewards to the users. If your company does not have a system such as this in place, it would definitely be worth looking into as it can save you both time and money by centralizing and standardizing the training process.

When selecting an LMS, consider if it is scalable for partners. Hosting training courses for external sales teams that are not part of your company is essential for ensuring that they also have the necessary tools and information to be successful. You may need to reduce or omit some of the information in the partner-focused courses to keep company confidential information safe but this is a small price to pay for including partners in your sales enablement process.

After an LMS is in place, courses can be created and administered to students. One way to do this is to organize courses into mandatory programs which are regularly scheduled to keep your students up to date with the latest information.

At one company, unique quarterly training programs were made mandatory for the different business units. For example, there would be a mandatory program called, "Sales Q3" or "Presales Q4". Each program consisted of hand-picked courses that best suited its audience. Part of my team's responsibility was to work with the course creators, collect their suggested courses for the upcoming quarter, and submit them to the Vice President of Presales for review and selection. We would then communicate which courses had been chosen to make sure that they were created before the beginning of the upcoming quarter.

After doing this manually the first time, we opted to simplify the process by setting up automatic reminders for the next four quarters. The course creators received a reminder six weeks before the new quarter was about to begin that reminded them to fill in a shared document with their intended courses. All we had to do at that point was link the document to the Vice President of Presales, wait to hear which courses had been chosen, and then communicate the results back to the course creators.

Another company did not use mandatory programs but rather placed the courses into categories. Here is a simplified version:

1. Onboarding

    a) Human Resources Introduction
    b) Company Tools
    c) Product Introduction

2. Continuous

    a) Product Updates and New Launches
    b) Sales-specific
    c) Marketing-specific

When a new employee joined the company, she would be required to complete a week of onboarding training through the LMS before flying to headquarters for a week of face-to-face training. After the second week, she would return home and receive continuous training courses as they became available such as when a new product was to be launched. This method ensured both a sound foundational base and continuous learning.

Onboarding with Playbooks
and Battlecards

During onboarding, a company may hand out a "Sales Playbook" to all new hires. This type of playbook can be a simple PDF document that is stored in the LMS and used to explain the basics of the company and industry, the different buyer personas, and the main competitors. While this approach can work for onboarding, it may be forgotten and lose its value after the employee has been at the company for a month or so. Additionally, it may simply be too much information for a new employee who is already coping with a new environment, colleagues, and product, and should be put off for a few weeks until they have settled in.

Another approach to creating a playbook is with the intention that it is a living document to be used as a reference point for discussions with prospects and customers. I have seen this approach executed extremely well although it does require maintenance work from various stakeholders. This type of playbook can take the form of an online database, a document with a table of contents at the beginning, or a printed booklet. Imagine it being structured to contain the next steps a salesperson should take in different scenarios. For example, an existing customer currently pays for Product Y but you would like to upsell Product A to them. The document has a section for customers who only have Product Y and contains an explanation for why adding Product A to their portfolio would benefit them, including up-to-date links to relevant content. As an example of what this content could be, perhaps the marketing team recently published a blog about Product A and the link to the blog is conveniently saved within this playbook so that immediately after the salesperson ends the call with the customer, they can simply copy and paste the link into a follow-up email.

Another useful onboarding technique is to create product-focused battlecards. An example would be a simple one-page PDF which includes the following elements:

1. Product Basics

2. Concise Sales Pitch

3. Key Questions for Customers (which highlight their pain points and the solutions you offer)

4. Frequently Asked Questions and Answers

5. Common Objections and Responses

Populating the Frequently Asked Questions and Answers and common objections and responses is best accomplished with input from your own Sales and Support teams. These are the people who come into the most contact with both prospects and existing customers. It is important to work with these groups as they typically handle the most product-related questions, objections, and requests.

Continuous Learning

Make sure that regardless of how product training is delivered, it occurs internally within your organization before the information reaches the outside world. I have seen too many times when customers or prospects read about a new feature from a piece of marketing content and yet when they asked a salesperson or Support Technician about it, that person was unable to provide them with the details because they had not been properly trained beforehand. This can be a very frustrating and embarrassing situation.

In reference to product release plans from the previous chapter, including training in the plan is an easy way to make sure that the training box is checked before a new product or feature is launched. Additionally, you may want to specify how the different release types determine who receives training and what the training content consists of. Here is an example:

	P1	P2	P3	P4
Business Units	• Entire Company	• Technical Support • CSM • BDM • Marketing	• Technical Support • CSM • BDM	• Technical Support • CSM
Exam	Yes	Yes	No	No
Training Content	• The PM creates a company-internal video explanation • The PMM creates a company-internal USP video • Technical documentation updates • Sales collateral updates • Social media links for public sharing	• The PM creates a company-internal video explanation • The PMM creates a company-internal USP video • Technical documentation updates • Sales collateral updates	• The PM creates a company-internal video explanation • Technical documentation updates	• The PM creates a company-internal video explanation

In the above example, four types of releases are accounted for. A P1 release requires that everyone in the company receive the training while a P4 only requires that the Technical Support and Customer Success Management teams be trained. Likewise, A P1 release will contain an exam and a significant amount of training content while the P4 release will not contain an exam or much content.

It is also the PMM's responsibility to train the company on the manner in which the product information will be communicated externally (e.g. through a webinar, a new product sheet, a press release, etc.) on the day of the launch so your teams know what to expect. You will also find that if you instruct your team on what is expected of them during the launch, they will be prepared. For example, instead of simply announcing, "We will host a webinar", you could say, "We will host a webinar targeted to existing customers. What you can do to help is to reach out to your existing customer base and invite them to attend. We have prepared an email template for you and our goal is to attain over two-hundred registrations."

Microlearning

Some of my favorite people to work with over the years have been in sales. They are easy to approach, positive, sociable, and remember something personal about you with which to start or continue a conversation. They also have a demanding job that requires all of their attention.

I used to work closely alongside the best salesperson I have ever met but for all of his strengths, he often turned to me for help with product information. He used to call me while he was traveling abroad and in meetings with customers and would start the conversation with, "Hello, my friend! I am sitting here with Company X and they have some product-related questions for you. By the way, you are on speakerphone."

While I was always happy to help him, I sometimes wondered why he could not remember all of the product details on his own. This example highlights how little time many salespeople have to focus on learning and remembering product details in comparison with someone like a PM or PMM whose role is very different.

This is where microlearning comes into play -- the delivery of bite-sized pieces of information that are easy to digest and remember. The PMM can impart the USP as well as the values and benefits of the product to the sales team and yet, not inundate them with too much information. They will be grateful to receive the information in this way, while still able to learn about the products on a more detailed level when they have the time.

The world of sales is fast moving and ever-demanding. Put yourself in their shoes and keep the message simple and to the point. Less is more so long as the crucial information is delivered. Empathy is the key. Although PMs and PMMs may have a lot of great information that they wish to convey to the world, it can quickly become too much for the sales team and prospects to handle at once.

One such example was a PMM I worked with who was a true expert of not only his product but of the industry. He would spend days putting all of his knowledge into presentations that were never shorter than fifty slides, each slide full to the brim with text. While this compilation of information was remarkable, it was simply too much to consume for anyone who was not solely focused on that product.

A clever salesperson in the company observed that this approach was not useful for empowering the sales team. Reading the document could take hours and was simply too pedantic to be useful. He found a solution by interviewing the PM with the most frequently asked product questions from customers and then adding the answers to a short sales guide that he had created on his own.

With all of the content created by different stakeholders, the PMM should always take the approach of keeping the message concise and full of value for the audience.

Document Management System

We have looked at implementing an LMS for training purposes but what about making material easy to find within your company and accessible outside of it? This is an issue I have struggled with for all types and sizes of organizations. While most companies already have a Document Management System (DMS) in place, it might be time to look into one if yours does not. However, it isn't enough to simply drop endless amounts of content into a large folder structure, hoping that salespeople will either remember the document locations based on emails you sent them during the past year or intuitively be able to find everything, and have the time to look for it, on their own.

As a PMM, it is important that you position yourself as a stakeholder in this discussion and decision-making process. As with the LMS, think about how scalable your solution is. If you have found a good solution for storing and sharing material internally, is it also accessible to partners? If yes, is there a way to partition it and keep the company confidential information for internal eyes only? How about the ability to share the sales and marketing material with prospects, customers, and other external organizations?

Another key factor for the PMM is tracking the usage of material that you and your marketing team generate. Without knowing what is accessed by your sales team and/or viewed and downloaded by prospects and customers, you have no way of knowing what material has been successful, widely used, or needs updating. Better yet, do you know specifically who viewed each document, which parts of it, and for how long? Likewise, you will be unaware of what material was less successful or used and should be archived.

Some companies use their DMS for internal use only, meaning that the material it contains is not accessible externally. This means that documents must be downloaded from the DMS, stored locally on a salesperson's computer, and then manually attached to emails for external sharing. If this is the case, the DMS most likely allows you to generate reports for which users have viewed and/or downloaded a certain document and when. Unfortunately, what you most likely will see is that someone has downloaded it just once many months ago and then never again. This is because they now keep it stored locally on their own computer. Besides the danger of this person not having the latest version of the document when it is updated in the DMS, you will have no visibility as to how many prospects they sent it to or if those prospects ever viewed it.

One solution, although not always the most effective one, is to simply ask your sales team how much they use the different documents by sending out a quarterly or annual survey. In the survey, you can list the material that has been created or updated during the last time period and ask them how often they used each document. You may have too much content to include in detail in the survey but even questions such as, "Have the three eBooks for Product Y been useful to you?" will shed some light on what the salespeople find useful. Adding open-ended questions in the survey is a good way to collect additional feedback on what can be improved. Better yet, spend some face-to-face time with them to ask them the same questions. There is a good chance that these sessions will identify documents that the salespeople were not aware of or were too busy to pay heed to when first informed about them.

I once worked for a very large organization that had offices worldwide, an LMS in place, a website with gated and ungated content, a popular DMS in use, etc. All of the tools were there but because there were so many employees, it was virtually impossible for anyone to find the documents they were looking for, be it internal material and documentation or links to externally sharable material.

My team was responsible for deciding how sales and marketing material was presented to the sales team, partners, prospects, and customers. Unfortunately, none of the tools that we had offered all of the functionality that we needed. The LMS was used by our partners but could not be used for sharing material externally with customers. The DMS was locked for internal use only and could not be used for sharing material with partners or customers. This meant that material for customers had to be shared via email or the website. While this is understandable because all of these solutions were developed and used for different purposes, it made it very difficult for our company to operate as a whole.

After much deliberation, we found the best solution; We created a directory in the root of the LMS called, "Sales Material". The material was not uploaded to the LMS directly and did not actually exist in this location because storing large amounts of files in an LMS is messy and not what it was designed for. Instead, we created subfolders titled, "Sales Decks", "eBooks", "White Papers", "Fact Sheets", and so on. Inside of each of those subfolders, we placed links that linked to our other systems (the website, DMS, etc.) Our rationale was that the sales team regularly accessed the LMS due to their continuous training programs so why not kill two birds with one stone by creating a section that could serve as a table of contents for the material they needed, regardless of the material's actual storage location?

It did not exactly work as planned. Many salespeople complained that one tool led to another, which was time-consuming and confusing to navigate. In addition, people from other business units liked the idea but then began to upload their material directly into the LMS, bypassing the DMS completely. Unfortunately, our project was unsuccessful and we were forced to search for yet another tool which was designed for sharing sales collateral externally with customers and tracking when and by whom it was viewed and downloaded.

Unless you can find a system that provides everything you need, you will need to compromise by using multiple tools. An LMS is great for training purposes and can scale to train and certify partners and customers but document storage and sharing is another story.

When organizing the contents of the DMS, keep the folder structure as simple and self-explanatory as possible and provide your sales team with cheat sheets such as a text file that contains links to all of the most used and shared external material. Tagging each document with relevant keywords and metadata is also an effective method that allows any salesperson to find what they are looking for through a simple search.

At the end of the day, you can never prevent salespeople from asking where a certain document is. The best you can do is make it as easy as possible for them to find what they need.

Recurring Knowledge Sharing Calls

A great method for continuously disseminating information and collecting feedback is to host regular (weekly, bi-weekly, monthly, etc.) company calls. These calls are essentially a recurring internal webinar designed for the sole purpose of keeping your sales team, and any other relevant teams, up to date with the latest product marketing news. These calls may need to be organized outside of the normal working hours to avoid disrupting the sales day. However, they can be recorded for anyone unable to attend them.

Soliciting various speakers (usually PMs or someone from development or marketing) to present their latest product updates is a great way to keep the sales team up to date without relying on emails, which have a good chance of being ignored. It is also a good idea to ask a particular salesperson to speak about how he recently signed a new customer, what process he went through, and who the gatekeepers and decision-makers were. Sales management is usually more than happy to see the best sales methods cloned through these shared experiences.

Having someone speak about the latest information on competitors is also useful and appreciated. Perhaps this can be tied into the new customer story, for example, "We were up against competitor X but eventually won the deal. Here is what we learned and what should be repeated next time."

Of course you can always leave a speaking slot for yourself to highlight some material or promote an upcoming event or product launch that your marketing and development teams have been working on.

Depending on the tool you use to host the calls, it can also be useful to conduct a poll during the session which typically yields a high response rate as your audience is focused and has the time to read and answer one or a few simple questions. Polls are a quick and easy way to gather feedback about any subject.

Additionally, sending a follow-up survey is a great way to receive additional feedback and improve future sessions. Typically, the three most important questions that need answering are the following:

1. How useful was this session for you? (slider scale)

2. How well did the presenters know and explain the material? (slider scale)

3. What ideas or suggested topics do you have for the next session? (Open-ended answer)

While hosting your own calls may be useful in larger organizations to make sure that your product marketing updates are communicated to the necessary audiences, it may be enough in smaller companies to occasionally join your sales team's regular team calls as a guest speaker. These typically take place to review targets, the pipeline, and achieved results but also to share best practices and success stories. They also provide you with the perfect opportunity to get a feel for the current sales climate and to pitch new material to the team.

Competitor Analysis

As you receive feedback through polls, surveys, and face-to-face sessions with your sales team, you will most likely encounter a common theme for more information about competitors. Competition is healthy, leads to growth and innovation, and should not be seen as a negative thing.

At one company, I traveled to trade shows all around the world to promote our products and support the local sales teams. After the first few trips, I became friends with my counterpart, another PMM, at one of our largest competitors who was attending the same events.

One of these events was the Mobile World Congress in Barcelona, Spain which I attended with a large group of my colleagues, including our CEO. The CEO asked two of us to check out that particular competitor and see if we could get a secret glimpse of their products. We set off towards their booth and as we approached, my colleague said, "Quick, hide your name tag and badge so that they don't know which company we are with." To my colleague's alarm, I left my name tag and the badge around my neck, went up to my PMM friend, and asked "What's new with your products this year?" He was glad to see me and agreed to show us their latest innovations if we would show him ours. Sure enough, he gave us an informative demo and in return, he visited our booth (much to the chagrin of my colleagues) where I showed him our brand new Graphical User Interface and the advantages it had.

I believe both companies profited from the experience that day and it was a much more professional way of going about it than purchasing each other's products online under a pseudonym or hiding our badges and going "under cover" at the trade show.

This is not to say that I have not also seen the petty side of competition. I once organized a webinar only to find out that two weeks before it was scheduled, one of our competitors scheduled a webinar on the exact same topic on the exact same day at the exact same time!

I also worked at many companies that endured constant disparaging comments from competitors as a sales technique. I was grateful when the CEO of one of those companies addressed our entire company and said, "It is absolutely unacceptable behavior to bad-mouth our competitors." Although positioning your company and its USP to win deals in competition is a natural part of the business, bad-mouthing is not professional and does not reflect well upon you or your company. Instilling these values in your sales and marketing teams is a great way for the PMM to act as a leader.

The PMM is heavily involved in competitor analysis and there are many great books written on this subject. At smaller companies, it may fall completely upon your shoulders. At larger companies, competitor analysis may reside in a Strategy or Research team but include the PMM as a stakeholder in the research and material creation.

Battlecards can once again be a smart way of conveying the information; each battlecard can be dedicated to a specific competitor or competitor's product and should provide the sales team with the proper comparisons and arguments.

As an example of what a battle card can contain, I have chosen to use the most extensive version that I have come across in my career. Not all of these fields may be necessary for your needs but this is a good place to begin:

- Company in a Nutshell
- Product Positioning
- Company Strengths
- Company Weaknesses
- Products/Services Overview
- Pricing
- Product Strengths
- Product Weaknesses
- Reasons Why They Win Against Us
- Reasons Why We Win Against Them
- What is Expected From Them When They Sell Against Us
- ATTACK (What topics to highlight when selling against this competitor)
- DEFEND (What topics you will need to defend when selling against this competitor)
- AVOID (What topics you should do your best to avoid when selling against this competitor)
- Supporting Links

If you want even more detailed information about a competitor, you can include additional fields such as:

- Office Locations
- Investors
- Latest Financial Information
- Number of Employees
- Partners
- Market Presence
- Customers
- Industries
- Sales Strategy

Competitor-specific company information can be obtained through their website, other online sources such as analyst reports or third-party reviews, interviews with employees who are new to your organization and who formerly worked for them (either directly or indirectly), interviews with their/your customers who have used or continue to use their products, and of course, testing out their products for yourself.

After you have collected the information, you need to position your company and its products in such a way that your sales team can win deals in competition. As the PMM, make sure that you focus your research on directly comparing their product and pricing with yours. Side-by-side comparison charts listing your product's features compared to theirs is a great place to start. Back this up with documentation containing screenshots of their product and detailed descriptions of how their product works.

Preparing a compelling argument for your pricing versus theirs is another invaluable and necessary way to prepare your sales team. They will constantly be required to explain price differences and if they are not equipped with persuasive arguments, they will lose deals and become demoralized.

Proactive RFP

Another useful tool to support a sales team is a "Proactive RFP", in which "RFP" stands for "Request For Proposal". The Proactive RFP is a spreadsheet with each tab dedicated to a specific product developed by that company. When I first encountered this tool, it was created by the PMM team but received constant updating and maintenance by the presales team.

There are two versions of the Proactive RFP; The first version consists solely of questions about the products while the second version also includes the answers to those questions. The question-only version was available for free download on our company's website and was linked to prospects who were considering purchasing one or more of our products. The version with answers was not publicly shared.

The objective was simple: When a prospect was ready to purchase, they could submit an RFP. The salesperson working with them would send the Proactive RFP and explain that our company was happy to help the prospect decide whether our product should be chosen over a competing one. The prospect was then encouraged to send the Proactive RFP with its list of questions to our competitors for responses to the questions.

The questions were both general and specific but they were also skewed to make our products appear to be the best choice. For example, if it were known that most competing products did not have a certain feature that our product did have, there would be a question, "Does your product have this feature?"

With the answer-version ready at hand, it would only take a few seconds for our sales team to send the answers to the prospect while the competitor's sales team would unsuccessfully struggle with the difficult questions.

Although this method worked well at that company, I have also seen simpler methods that were equally effective. On one occasion, a colleague of mine showed me an email she received in which the sender, who was trying to sell her a service, had included five simple product-related questions in the body of the email that highlighted our need for their service, and at the same time, set itself apart from their competition.

ROI Calculators

A common practice is for the PMM team to create and maintain various ROI calculators that the sales team can use directly with prospects to determine exactly how much cost savings the products would generate for their companies. ROI calculators are usually created in spreadsheets and built so that a salesperson can sit down together with a prospect and fill in the blank fields until the form is complete and the full ROI is revealed.

As a simple example, a calculator could determine how much a company would save by moving from on-premise servers to the Cloud. In this situation, some of the fields in the calculator might include the following:

1. How many on-premise servers do you currently have?

2. What is your monthly spend for the power and cooling of each server?

3. What is your monthly spend for encryption, firewall, and other security measures installed on each server?

4. What is your monthly spend for the hypervisor and application licenses installed on each server?

5. What is your monthly spend for IT Administrators and other staff to maintain the servers and their applications?

The calculator would display how much the prospect currently spends on hosting their own server environment and then compare that to the much lower cost of moving everything to the Cloud with SaaS applications and licensing.

ROI calculators can transform the prospect into an internal salesperson at their own company. If your salesperson can use solid numbers to prove cost savings, the prospect may suddenly see an opportunity to shine in his own organization by pushing your solution to his decision-makers. He can take the ROI calculator to his boss and say, "Look at the wonderful product that I found. If we adopt it, our company will save THIS much!"

Demo Environments

Although numbers and potential cost savings are a strong message, seeing is believing. The PMM should be involved in equipping the sales team with the ability to demonstrate the products and deliver the core value-proposition.

As an example, one company I worked at was fully committed to live demonstrations of their products and had equipped their sales team to carry out demos on their own. Multiple online demo environments were created and maintained and could be reserved and used by one salesperson at a time. Additionally, they cloned the same environments and made them available for download. Many salespeople preferred using the offline method so they could run the environment in their own local Virtual Machine while visiting a prospect or customer.

Meanwhile, the PMM team stepped in to ensure that the corresponding presentation slides and/or speeches by the sales team focused on the values and benefits of the products rather than only their functionality and features. It was our job to deliver the proper training and supporting material to the salespeople so that whomever was on the receiving end of the product demonstrations would find the presentations engaging and would have a clear understanding of the problems our products would solve for them. We also offered different versions of the presentations as the messaging we created was tailored to each of the different buyer personas. This enabled the sales team to switch presentations or swap out slides depending on whom they were speaking with and to deliver the most value during their sales pitch and live demo of the products. When the discussion became more technical, a member of the Presales team was included to support the salesperson.

Flowcharts

While live demonstrations are indispensable, there are other ways for salespeople to act as consultants and lead the sales discovery process.

On occasion, I have seen PMMs involved in the creation of call scripts, designed to assist salespeople with exactly what to say. While this method may work for some companies, I have always found it rather dry as it does not leave much room for improvisation, personalization, or of course the most important of all sales skills: listening.

As an alternative to call scripts, a product flowchart may be useful as a sales conversion tool. As an example, the first product flowchart that I created originated from a Technical Support Manager who was looking for a method to make it easier for his team to identify which product was the best solution for the customer's needs. Our software was highly reliant upon what kind of hardware that was used and the Support staff would often receive questions from the sales team about which product to offer for which kind of hardware.

The flowchart they used was a simple wireframe, displaying which products fell under which hardware types. I requested access to the editable document and created a sales-friendly version as seen below:

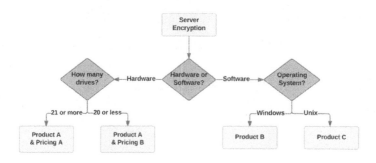

Our actual product offering was much more complex and could lead to many different combinations of products for a satisfactory solution. If your product offering is rather simple, this type of flowchart can be useful to help your sales team become comfortable with it. If it is more complex, your sales team may find value in continuously referring to it to avoid unnecessarily consulting their technical teams.

With all of these tools, processes, and training, your sales and marketing teams are more than ready to deliver their message to the world. The next question is: *What is that message?*

V

PRODUCT POSITIONING AND MESSAGING

We've made it to the heart of product marketing! Leaving the interaction with other business units aside, let's take a look at what lies at the very center of being a PMM: Positioning your products with the right messaging to reach and appeal to your target audiences, highlight your USP, and create a clear differentiation from the competition.

To reach the right positioning, you need to first understand your target audience, the problems they are trying to solve, and how they will go about finding and evaluating your products. What it all comes down to, regardless of what methodology you use to understand your buyers, is that you know the "Why" that fuels their interest in your products.

They are interested in your product, but why? They have pain points and problems which need solving, but why? Following the "Why" down to the right level of understanding will help form your positioning and messaging so that you can speak directly to what they are looking for and why your product is the right choice.

There are various ways to understand to whom you are trying to sell. The traditional method is to create buyer personas for everyone in your company to refer to in a simple and standardized way. Buyer personas are a representation of the different types of prospects and customers your company sells to. They are created through market research and the use of data that has been collected about your customers.

Yet another method is to use Jobs To Be Done in which personas are irrelevant because the focus is on what the users of your products are trying to achieve, rather than who they are. For example, with Jobs To Be Done, the exceptionally different demographics of two buyer personas do not matter because both are trying to accomplish the same thing with your product in a similar fashion. However, it can also be argued that while Jobs To Be Done indeed renders user personas irrelevant, buyer personas are still necessary to reach different types of buyers and assist them through their decision-making process, which is still quite a varied experience.

It is up to you and your company to decide how to identify and cater to your different buyers and users. There is already a lot of great material on both personas and Jobs To Be Done but let's cover some of the basics.

Buyer Personas

If you are new at a company or have been there for some time but have only recently begun to develop personas, it is advisable to ask the managers of other business units if personas have already been created by their teams. The development team may already have user personas in place for describing how various types of users (Admins, Managers, Users) interact in their own way with the products. You may also discover that the marketing team has their own buyer personas for identifying the kind of marketing and sales material and communication methods that work best with different people. If more than one set of personas exists within your company, it might be beneficial to align them. Selling to and designing a product for an IT Administrator who works at a startup as opposed to a non-technical manager who works for a branch of the government and is conducting a public tender to find the right product will differ greatly in the eyes of both your marketing and development teams. The marketing team will use different methods of communication and types of material to sell to the IT Administrator and to the government manager. Likewise, the development team will take the two very different persona requirements into consideration when designing the product. The IT Administrator is probably accustomed to working with technical functionality while the non-technical manager requires a simple user interface.

Consulting with the different teams in your company and agreeing upon a common set of personas makes sense so that when someone from the development team refers to one of their user personas, let's say "John" as an example, their counterpart in the marketing team knows to whom they are referring. The marketing team will establish how to communicate with John while the development team will identify John by how he interacts with the products, but at least there is common ground.

Whether your company is Business-to-Business (B2B) or Business-to-Consumer (B2C) will obviously play a large part in the definition and outcome of your personas. Likewise, conducting research to define your personas can be done in a variety of different ways. Speaking with and interviewing both customers and prospects is an obvious option and can be done individually or in groups. Using and listening to social media, checking profiles on professional networking sites, sending surveys, and speaking with your sales and support teams to better understand the daily problems and requests of your customers and prospects are also common methods of research.

The level of detail and complexity of your finalized personas will vary on a company-by-company basis. There may be a need for multiple pages to cover topics such as:

1. Profile

2. Initial reasons and drive to search for a new solution

3. Expected results from your product

4. Perceived barriers

5. Decision criteria

Condensing the most relevant information onto a single page is optimal to increase the odds that your colleagues will actually read it. A longer version can still play a role, for example when reading five pages of information for one persona for a specific research project, but one page should suffice to convey the most important information, as a general rule. After the personas are complete, identifying which ones are relevant at the beginning of every meeting is a good way to ensure that everyone knows whom you are targeting with each project.

Let's take a look at four key elements when building a buyer persona.

1. Begin with demographics: Age, sex, location, etc. These are all important in understanding more about who they are and where they come from. This will also help define the language you use when marketing and selling to them. Demographics are especially important when it comes to B2C. In a B2B company, it is often the roles that you are targeting that are important, such as General Manager, CEO, IT Administrator, etc.

2. Build out their identities in a search for what drives them to look for and purchase a product. Purchasing is often in part an emotional decision so understanding what motivates them is crucial. For B2C, do they have children, what level of education did they reach, what is their annual income, etc. For B2B, are they a decision-maker in their organization? What type of budget might they have to work with? What other motivations might they have? For example, will they look good in the eyes of their boss if they discover and present the right product or solution?

3. Now it's time to identify their pain points. What problem do they currently have that your product will solve? Does this problem affect them daily? Don't settle for just what they want but understand why it matters. "When X, I want to Y, so that I can Z."

4. Finally, how can you reach your different personas? Do some of them read lengthy analyst reports while

others scroll quickly through social media channels? Does one of them download technical white papers while another simply wants a call from one of your salespeople? The tone of voice, amount of detail, and methods of communication that you use to speak to your different personas determine whether or not they will hear and understand your message clearly.

Buyer's Journey

Now that we know to whom we are selling and what motivates them to purchase your product, we need to understand the buyer's journey.

Awareness, consideration, and decision. These are the three main stages that any buyer must go through before purchasing a product or service. Typically, companies extend and customize these three stages to create their own specific buyer's journey. For example, many software companies add a "Trial/Evaluation" stage between the Consideration and Decision phases.

A PMM team that I belonged to built something akin to the chart below. In it, every one of the company's buyer personas was listed on the left column while the seven stages of their purchasing our products were on the top. For this example, I have kept the original three stages.

	Awareness	Consideration	Decision
General Manager	Sales Deck #1 White Paper #1 Marketing Video #1	Analyst Report #1 Case Study #1 Product Sheet #1	Demo Deck #1 Tutorial Video #3
Chief Financial Officer	Sales Deck #2 Analyst Report #1 Marketing Video #1	ROI Calculator #1 Analyst Report #2 Marketing Video #2	ROI Calculator #2 Case Study #3
IT Administrator	Sales Deck #3 Tutorial Video #1 eBook #1	Product Sheet #2 Tutorial Video #2 Case Study #2	Demo Deck #2

The sales team would refer to this chart when searching for the most relevant material to send to the different personas, depending upon their current stage in the buyer's journey.

Although this method may still be applicable, the buyer's journey can be rather fragmented. Buyers are increasingly more independent when searching for and finding a product, educating themselves about it, comparing it to similar products, and purchasing it. For example, a prospect may browse your website with their smartphone and view a particular product page and then a few days later, use their tablet for another visit to read some additional material or read that same product page again. A week later, they may purchase the product on their computer. Different touch points and engagements make it more difficult to track the number of interactions and the flow of the journey from awareness to consideration to decision.

A good beginning to understanding the buyer's journey is identifying the keywords and trends that your prospects are searching for. Again, this is where keyword planning tools can be helpful. Additionally, send out surveys and interview customers about how they found and chose your product. They may not remember specifics, such as when and how they first came into contact with your product, but this doesn't mean they won't be able to provide you with useful insights.

Your sales team may not be involved in the buyer's journey at all. The better your product marketing, the more this is possible.

On one occasion, I found six similar SaaS products to meet a requirement of my company. To select the best product, I first read online reviews and ratings from other users to better compare the products and understand which would best suit our needs. Thanks to the reviews and ratings, I narrowed my search to three of the six products. I briefly browsed the websites of each of these three products and read what they had to tell me about functionality and pricing. Having found that they were all on par with one another after this phase, I watched tutorial videos to see what the products actually looked like.

One of these companies offered only ten-minute videos which took too long to get to the point and didn't do a good job highlighting the values and benefits that I would want should I choose its product. The other two companies had relevant, short, and to-the-point videos which showcased beautiful products that appeared to offer all of the functionality that I required.

With the two remaining choices, I clicked on "Free Trial" for both of them and tested the user experience by creating the real-life scenario that my company would encounter when using this product. One of the products had helpful tips built into the user interface and a logical workflow; the other was less helpful to me as a new user.

Having now made my choice, and after checking the pricing one final time, I paid a significant amount of money to the company that I believed would provide us with a valuable product. At no point during that buyer's journey did I speak with a sales or support representative from any of those six companies.

Today's buyers have access to so much information from so many different sources, that it is the company that provides quick access to the right messaging that wins the sale. As someone progresses through the buyer's journey, more lengthy material such as a technical white paper or analyst's research report may become relevant for a particular persona but getting them to that point is only possible if you capture their attention from the beginning.

It is also important to look at it from the perspective of the marketing funnel. Ideally, the material that you create will be viewed in the order that you wish and therefore, it is important to consider where it fits into the funnel. Will this particular piece of content be seen by someone who has discovered your company for the first time, someone who has already shown interest in your offering but needs more prompting, or by someone who is already on the verge of purchasing your product? Depending on where in the marketing funnel a particular piece of content will live, it is worth considering whether it should be gated or not. If it is gated, that means the person who wishes to view it must input information about themselves (typically name and email address) in order to access and download it. While it wouldn't make much sense to gate a success story, it would be advisable to gate an eBook to obtain new leads. Wouldn't you feel put-off if you wanted to read how a product had helped another company similar to yours and yet you did not have open and immediate access to that material? That information should not be difficult to obtain if you are in market to purchase a product. On the other hand, if you wish to read an eBook about best practices in your industry, providing your email address is a small price to pay for a free download.

Work closely with your content marketing and demand generation teams to understand how the funnel has been mapped out for your company and what material and activities work best for moving prospects through it. As an example, the funnel will typically contain these elements:

Top of the funnel

- Paid ads

- eBooks

- Educational webinars

Middle of the funnel

- Case studies

- Product sheets

- Tutorial videos

Bottom of the funnel

- Free trial

- Live demo

- Consultation

As prospects get closer to the bottom of the funnel, the voice of the PMM should only get louder. This is where your messaging and unique positioning plays a crucial role in closing the sale. When you feel confident in your material, are you aware of how prospects find and navigate through your website to access it? Some good questions are:

- From where do visitors come when they first land on your company's website (a search engine, a paid advertisement of yours that they clicked on, a direct input of your company's web address into the browser)?

- What is the bounce rate of visitors who land on your homepage only to click back to their previous page and leave without exploring your site further? This can be a clear indication of how well your messaging is working.

- How long do they spend on any given page before moving on to the next?

- Which pages lead most frequently to other pages?

Following a fragmented buyer's journey from start to finish may not always be possible but any metrics you can obtain and analyze are extremely useful. There are useful software tools designed specifically for tracking how visitors navigate through your website.

Another exercise is to watch prospects and customers navigate through your website as they search for specific information. This can be accomplished in person or by joining them on a call in which you can both view and record their screens. Customers might be familiar with your company and at least one of your products but perhaps you would like to upsell another product that they don't know much about. At the beginning of a call, pitch the new product and then ask them to find more information about it online. It can be challenging to get prospects to do this, but if you can watch while they search for information online about what your product does, you will see the paths they take.

In both cases:

- How do they find their way to your homepage, product page, or landing page?

- Do they encounter outdated links or material along the way?

- Is the specific information they are looking for easy to find and is the messaging clear enough that they don't need to stop to ask you a question?

As my colleagues and I have conducted these sessions, we have seen clear trends from both prospects and customers. For example, after someone finds the product page they are looking for, they usually do not want to leave that page to find additional information. That means that a completely separate page that lists the pricing for all of your different products may not be optimal if you can put specific pricing for each product onto the product pages themselves. Equally, if navigating to a "Resources" page is the only way to view customer testimonials and success stories, it might be prudent to move at least a few of them to the product pages or link directly to them. Ask your sales team to organize these calls for you. It takes no more than ten minutes per call but can lead to invaluable insights into both your buyer's journey and product messaging.

Following awareness, consideration, and decision, the buyer's journey extends into the use of your product, and finally into customer loyalty and advocacy. As we saw in the search for the right SaaS product example, human interaction may never actually take place which means that your product needs to market itself. Just like with the marketing team's reports, can your development team produce reports for you that map the user's journey? What tabs or buttons do they click on and in which order? With what other external systems do they connect your product via API?

Identify these key points of interaction and use them to your advantage. A few examples include:

- Place links to helpful tutorial videos and documentation in the appropriate places.

- A/B test different word choices for keeping a user interested in a certain functionality or making them aware of its existence.

- Make it clear that you have technology partnerships with other companies in your ecosystem.

What it all comes down to is putting yourself in your buyer's shoes so you can produce the right messaging and positioning and tell a compelling story.

Company Internal Research

When looking at the big picture of what your product line achieves as a whole, product positioning can extend all the way to company and brand positioning. Establishing this positioning will require the input and approval of all key stakeholders in your company, including the C-level. When positioning a single product, the PMM will consult all relevant stakeholders but should have the autonomy to make the final decisions.

Regardless of whether you are in the process of positioning the entire product line or a single product, if you were to walk through your office and randomly pick a person from each business unit, could they answer the following questions? More importantly, would they all have the same answers?

1. Using no more than five words, what is your product offering?

2. What is the elevator pitch to expand upon the first question?

3. What are some differentiation points that set our product apart from its competition?

Educating everyone in your company to produce the same answers for these three basic questions is a huge victory for any PMM. Bear in mind that due to different perspectives within the company, this can be a difficult task. Opinions invariably differ on what should be communicated about your products and services. For example, different buzzwords and messaging may attract attention in different sales verticals or regions and a salesperson who caters to the Small and Medium Business segment will have different expectations than a salesperson who targets larger companies.

When it comes to defining positioning and messaging, I have found that speaking with the developers is the best place to begin. These are the people who will explain to you exactly what it is that the products or solutions accomplish and how they work technically. The answers from this team will be straight-forward and honest. Quite often, they will also tell you what the products should eventually be, but are not yet, capable of. As I have asked developers to review the existing sales collateral with me to help me better understand the current positioning, they often informed me that some of the messaging is on the verge of overpromising or is flat-out incorrect and there has been a disconnect between development and marketing. This is a wonderful place to begin the journey so that all of the positioning and messaging that you build will have a solid and credible foundation.

Next, work your way through to the PMs who have more interaction with the customers than the developers typically have. They will voice strong opinions and will lay out their big picture roadmaps of the future direction of the products.

Involving top management is a logical next step. Not only are many of these people your key stakeholders but they may be aware of future development plans for your company or products which need to be taken into consideration when crafting new positioning and messaging. You want to avoid launching your new positioning and messaging only to have to revise it again in six or twelve months due to major roadmap changes that even the PMs may not have foreseen. Top management will need to inform you of any bigger plans so that you can work together with that long-term vision in mind.

Next, chat with marketing. These are the people who create the content year after year and may have insights on how to better package the messaging.

By the time you get to the sales team, you will have a good grasp of how your company understands and views itself and will be ready to hear how its products are externally communicated and sold. This is the department in which you will hear the latest buzzwords and sales pitches used by sales team to hit their sales targets. Some of these people will follow the messaging and material provided at the outset of their time at your company, and yet others will create their own messaging and material to help them win deals their way. These are also the people who most often come up against competition and should have a good understanding of how competitors position their products. Inquire why they use the words and methods they have chosen to win the deals. Are competitors using those same words and finding success? Did a salesperson find and read an inspirational article that offered an explanation of how to solve the problems of your industry's needs? Did another salesperson simply come up with a great idea for positioning on their own?

Competitor Positioning

Having spoken with everyone in your organization, the next step is to look at how competitors position themselves. Keeping an eye on competition should be a continuous exercise and source of information.

Some examples include:

- What messaging do they use on their website's homepage?

- Have they coined a term or phrase that always lists their website first when entered into a search engine?

- How is their product line broken down into individual products?

- Is their pricing transparent? If so, how does it

compare with yours?

- What do their customer success stories look like and what is the focus of their messages?

- What is their call to action? (e.g. free trial, live demo, etc.)

In addition, look at the big picture of all of your competitors. Is there a similarity of buzzwords that seem to be used by most of them? They are also reacting to the market, striving for the best Search Engine Optimization results, and A/B testing different options to increase their traffic and conversions. However, when a certain positioning or messaging is successful in a particular industry, it may be that everyone must adopt it to stay in the game.

In one situation, it was necessary for me to use the word, "certified" in my company's product positioning and messaging. Every competitor was using that particular word because third-party certifications were one of the main reasons relied upon by a prospect to select a company and its product. It quickly became a race (which we eventually won) with our competition to see which of us could acquire the most certifications.

In the best case scenario, your company will find new and unique positioning and messaging to enable it to become an industry leader. On the other hand, tweaking an already proven and widely accepted positioning to fit your company's USP is a viable alternative.

Though marketing the specific pricing of your products may not be optimal or possible, highlighting certain aspects of the pricing model might be used to great advantage. For example, does your company offer a free trial before someone is required to purchase? If not, does it provide them with an environment in which they can test the products, thereby bypassing the need for integration with their own live environment? Do you offer special promotions or offers?

Prospect and Customer Research

A common technique for keeping in touch with your buyers is to conduct regular Win/Loss interviews in which you call prospects who have been working with one of your salespeople and who recently decided to purchase or not purchase your product. Speaking with them will provide you with a window into their decision-making processes, budget constraints, explanations about why your product was or was not right for them, etc. Be sure to include messaging-related questions in the interview to provide insight into what exactly it was that the prospects were looking for in a product and how your messaging met, or did not meet, their requirements. Besides relying on your sales team to let you know when a significant deal has been won or lost, setting up notifications in your CRM system is an easy way to track these results.

In addition to Win/Loss interviews, organize calls or face-to-face discussions with your customers and prospects to dig deeper into the product marketing aspect of their decision-making process. Focus groups are also a useful method for sparking new discussion topics and uncovering consensus or disagreements among buyers.

Make sure that you reach out to a wide range of buyers such as:

1. Existing customers:

   a) Those who are pleased with your products and services.

   b) Those who are on the verge of churning. In other words, customers who are for one reason or another, considering switching to a competitor for the same functionality or to develop it in-house.

   c) Those who use one or more of your products

   d) Those who use a different mix of your product line than the others.

2. Prospects with whom your sales team is currently speaking but who have not yet decided to purchase your product.

3. Churned customers.

Note that when forming focus groups, you should avoid including the wrong types of buyers in the same room. For example, allowing a churned customer to speak with a prospect may have a negative impact on the prospect's decision-making process.

Additionally, if you bring a group of your customers together to ask them a series of questions, some of them may disagree with the answers given by others but might not have the courage to speak up in a group and therefore, will appear as though they agree. In this situation, a good practice is to ask everyone to write their answers down before the sharing begins to increase the odds that they will voice their opinions.

When speaking with your buyers, ask them open-ended questions and be careful not to put words in their mouths to avoid skewing the answers. Here are some sample questions that can help develop your positioning and messaging:

1. What were you initially searching for when you found our company/product?

2. What specific problems were you trying to solve and why?

3. What keywords did you input into the search engine?

4. Using no more than five words, what does our company/product do?

5. Did you choose us over a competitor? If yes, why?

If permitted, record these sessions and transcribe them later. This allows you to involve yourself in a meaningful discussion and probe for deeper explanations rather than focus on taking notes and perhaps missing out on key elements of the session.

Creating Your Product Positioning and Messaging

After you have collected information from both your colleagues and buyers, it is time to sculpt your positioning and messaging. Again, it all comes down to the "Why?" Use the information you gathered from speaking with your prospects and customers and turn it back on them to address their "Why?" When considering the buyer's needs, why would someone search for your product in the first place? What problem are they trying to solve or what task are they trying to make easier/faster?

I formerly worked with a salesman based in London who consistently delivered the best sales results in our organization, year after year. At that point in my career, I was insistent that all salespeople receive detailed product information and training as I believed that was the best contribution I could make to increase our sales. However, this particular salesman ignored the training and information that I provided, no matter how much I tried to convince him that it would be useful. I finally asked him why he was outright avoiding what I had to tell him about our products and his response was, "Frankly, I don't want to know the details of our products. When I call someone for the first time, I identify their problem and then provide the solution. Sometimes they are already aware of the problem and sometimes I have to bring it to their attention. Either way, I could be selling mattresses just as well as software." It was a good lesson for me -- to focus on a buyer's perspective of finding solutions to problems rather than to create messaging that only highlighted the amazing features our products had to offer.

When creating sales and marketing material, determine the percentage that should be persuasive and the percentage that should be descriptive. The persuasive parts will speak to the "Why?" as in: Why should someone request a demo of my product, consider switching from one of my competitor's products, or purchase it? The descriptive parts will address the "What?" and "How?" and enforce the persuasive arguments. Keep in mind that these percentages may fluctuate depending on the type of content. For example, a product sheet may be quite "What?" and "How?" focused while the homepage of your website may be almost entirely about the "Why?"

When creating messaging for existing customers, for example release notes for product updates, emphasize why they should pay attention to the latest changes made to the product. How will these updates affect them and why is it relevant that they be aware of them?

The messaging that your prospects and customers first come into contact with should focus on their emotional and aspirational goals and align with your brand and its values. The messaging they encounter later on can focus in more detail on your product and its features. This multilayered messaging is crucial to not only capture and hold their attention and drive them to purchase your product, but to separate your company from its competitors through unique positioning. It avoids the situation in which your company can only differentiate itself from its competitors by engaging in an endless feature war.

When drafting the final copy of your messaging, always be clear and never assume that everyone who reads it will have as much knowledge and experience as you do. A good place to start is with the naming of your products. If they are part of the same product line, do they, or should they, adhere to the same naming convention? Also keep an eye on the use of acronyms. I have had to learn new acronyms every time I joined a new company or switched industries. People who already work in those industries simply assume that everyone else will be familiar with those particular acronyms. However, we cannot assume that prospects, even those within our industry, are familiar with standard industry acronyms or especially those that are specific to our company and products. By avoiding the use of acronyms or by making sure that they have been explained, you can improve your messaging to everyone.

Clear messaging is important. If, for example, the landing page for one of your products states something akin to, "We empower companies of all sizes to unlock value through our scalable and reliable (no downtime) solution which harnesses the power of Big Data and the Internet of Things", no one will understand what it is that your product actually does. In fact, the reader may even feel offended, annoyed, or embarrassed, having not understood what you are trying to tell them.

Highlight your USP in the messaging by using information about your competitors. What do you do differently or better than they do? Does your company have patents it can boast about? What sets you apart from the others?

After you have created your initial messaging, work together with a graphic designer to build mock-ups of the first version (e.g. website homepage, presentation slides, one-pagers, etc.) and then test it. Run everything past your key internal stakeholders and collect feedback that will lead to a second version.

Next, get the new version to prospects and customers and gauge the results. Is the sales team having an easier time explaining what it is that your company and products do? Are prospects responding more favorably to the new material? Is the new positioning attracting more prospects and generating more demand for your products? Are competitors copying what you have done? These are all positive signs.

Successfully positioning your company and its products is an incredible accomplishment that impacts everyone in your organization. However, once you have accomplished what you set out to achieve, the journey doesn't end there. Perhaps you started by positioning your entire product line and can now focus on the messaging for each of the individual products, one by one. Perhaps the opposite.

Product positioning and messaging is an ongoing process and will need to be continuously revisited and updated. There are many reasons for repositioning, such as to reflect the changing attributes of one of your products or to target a new market or group of buyers that your company has decided to pursue. However, the more in-tune you are with your buyer personas and the buyer's journey, the more natural this process will feel.

CONCLUSION

Market Requirements Document

Everything that we have covered in this book can now be used to create a "Market Requirements Document", also sometimes referred to as a "Market Strategy Document". This is something that will require coordination with your colleagues to complete but, once done, will serve as a blueprint for your company's product marketing strategy. The ability to create such a document reflects your mastery of the topics within and highlights the value that you bring to your company on many levels.

Companies are all different and will expect this document to contain various types of data. Having said that, a good outline is as follows:

1. An executive summary of the document and its contents

2. Target customers and markets

3. Unique selling proposition, positioning, and messaging

4. Distribution plan and partners

5. Pricing, product offers, and promotions

6. Sales and marketing collateral

7. Online marketing strategy (Search Engine Optimization, paid ads, social media, etc.)

8. Conversion strategy

9. Customer referrals

10. Customer retention strategy

11. Financial projections

Final Thoughts

As buyers become even more independent and marketing departments produce material which results in direct sales, the role of the Product Marketing Manager will only become more relevant and in demand. Launching new products and features, building unique positioning, and creating multilayered messaging is not only the path to success, it is the most rewarding part of the journey.

I hope that this book has inspired you to begin or continue your career in the field of product marketing and provided the concepts and tools to help you succeed in it.

Happy product marketing!

Made in the USA
Las Vegas, NV
30 October 2022